P9-CMQ-910

COLD HARD TRUTH ON

FAMILY, KIDS & MONEY

COLD HARD TRUTH ON
FAMILY, KIDS
& MONEY

KEVIN O'LEARY

Doubleday Canada

Copyright © 2013 Kevin O'Leary

All rights reserved. The use of any part of this publication, reproduced, transmitted in any form or by any means electronic, mechanical, photocopying, recording or otherwise, or stored in a retrieval system without the prior written consent of the publisher—or in the case of photocopying or other reprographic copying, license from the Canadian Copyright Licensing Agency—is an infringement of the copyright law.

Doubleday Canada and colophon are registered trademarks of Random House of Canada Limited

Library and Archives Canada Cataloguing in Publication is available upon request
ISBN: 978-0-385-68240-4
eBook ISBN: 978-0-385-68241-1

This book is a story about building a family and financial dynasty; it represents my personal opinions and experiences. None of the content, anecdotes, stories, advice or recollections contained in this book should be construed as investment advice, especially as they relate to any financial products I may represent. Investors should speak with their financial advisors for any investment advice and to discuss the risks of investing in any financial product.
—Kevin O'Leary

Printed and bound in the USA

Published in Canada by Doubleday Canada,
a division of Random House of Canada Limited,
a Penguin Random House Company

www.randomhouse.ca

10 9 8 7 6 5 4 3 2 1

I dedicate this book to the anonymous nine-year-old girl who ran up to me in the San Francisco airport and told me she was going to be an entrepreneur so she could set her family free.

CONTENTS

ABOUT THIS BOOK

I crafted this book after a lifetime of working with money and developing an understanding of all the good and bad it can bring. In life we learn from our mistakes, but no mistake is more costly than a financial one. We teach our children about math, geography, science and even sex, but we forget to teach them about money. Money can become your most powerful ally or, if mistreated, your worst enemy. The key to financial success is developing from an early age a healthy relationship with money. Learn why it's there, where it comes from and what it means to borrow it. Above all, develop a respect for money, because it is impossible to live without it.

This is not a book about how to get rich overnight; there are no tricks of the trade in here that let you jump the line to prosperity. This book will help you successfully survive your journey with money and end up in a safe place where you can support yourself in your later years and perhaps help those you love, even after you are gone.

I don't care if you are nine years old or ninety, if you are just starting your career or have been retired for years, if you are single, married or divorced—the financial advice in this book works. Read it, follow it and you will make it to a place of security, health and happiness. I should know. I've already taken this journey.

—Kevin O'Leary

STRENGTHENING YOUR
FAMILY DYNASTY

For the past 15 years, our friends—we'll call them the Claytons—have hosted Thanksgiving dinner at their house. We always look forward to it. The tradition began when our kids were still small; Mitchell and Judy invited us and three other families to partake in their annual feast. Every year, my wife, Linda, and I pile in the car with our two children, Savannah and Trevor, and a couple bottles of good wine. When we get to the Claytons', the house is filled with people, laughter and the mouthwatering aroma of the turkey Judy has roasted to perfection yet again. The Claytons have it all—a beautiful home, two great kids, the perfect family and financial security.

At least they *did*, until the year everything fell apart.

Last Thanksgiving, we knew something was wrong the minute we pulled into the driveway. For starters, there weren't any other cars. "What's going on?" Trevor asked. We were all asking ourselves the same question.

I rang the bell and Mitchell came to the door. He looked like he had aged 12 years in 12 months. Linda and I had heard through some friends that he and Judy had been having some marital trouble, but to be perfectly honest, I didn't quite know how bad things had gotten. Judy and Mitchell had what looked to everyone like a wonderful relationship. They'd been married for decades and had such a great family that I immediately dismissed the rumors. But when I got to that door and saw Mitchell's face, I realized that things had gotten pretty bad—as bad as they can get.

"Come in, come in," he said, ushering us inside. "I'll introduce you to Meredith."

Meredith? Linda shot me a glance and grabbed my arm.

Sitting at the table, in Judy's normal place, was a woman who looked under 30 years old. She flashed a megawatt smile and gushed about how she'd heard so much about us from Mitchell and how happy she was to meet us. At the far end of the table was Elliott, the Claytons' grown son, looking sullen. Their daughter, Elise, was absent.

"Where's Elise?" Savannah asked.

Mitchell looked at his feet. "Elise couldn't make it home this year. Says she's studying hard at university and that she was busy. The other families couldn't make it, either, I'm afraid, which is why I'm so grateful you guys didn't back out on me." Mitchell finally found the courage to look up, and when he met my eye, I could see he was fighting back tears. Here was a man I'd known for years, a man who had had a solid family and, unbeknownst to me until that very moment, had seen it all fall apart in just a few months. How? Why? Nothing made any sense.

We approached the dining-room table where Meredith was sitting in Judy's place. Nobody asked about Judy. It was pretty clear she wouldn't be in attendance. The table was about as sad a sight as we'd ever seen. Normally, Judy created a gorgeous centerpiece with autumn wildflowers and maple leaves collected from their stunning property. Each person at the table usually had a name card made just for them, with a funny saying on it or cartoons drawn by Elise and Elliott. Not this year. The table was bare.

The whole night was a disaster. The house was eerily silent, so different from the boisterous joy of previous holidays. Elliott couldn't bring himself to sit down at the dinner table and was sitting off to the side in the living room, texting on his cell phone—something Judy would *never* have allowed. Meanwhile, Trevor had taken control of Elliott's video game console, and instead of hanging out with Elliott and talking a mile a minute with each other the way they usually did, each of them was in his own world. As for the "feast," Meredith and Mitchell had called a caterer, and Meredith, who had clearly never entertained guests in her entire life, was stressing about how to reheat the food she'd ordered. Linda stepped in and tried to help, but when she tried to initiate conversation, she came to the sudden realization that she had absolutely nothing in common with this younger, superficial woman. Linda and I later agreed dinner wasn't the only thing that year that was tasteless.

After dinner, I wandered to the picture window and looked out on the backyard. A cold drizzle fell against the windowpane, making the situation inside even more depressing. The flowers

Judy usually tended were dead in their beds. I looked again at Mitchell, who had huge, dark bags under his eyes. He said he was happy, but it was obvious the guy was a wreck. Despite the rain, Mitchell and I stepped outside for a moment and he proceeded to tell me how this had been the worst year of his life, that he'd made some serious errors in judgment and that, in the process, he'd lost everything he ever cared for—namely, his family. "I wanted to call and warn you that Judy wasn't going to be here," he said. "But it was all just so difficult and I couldn't find the words. Kevin," he said with one hand on my shoulder, "what have I done?"

I had no idea what to say to my friend. I couldn't believe my eyes. I couldn't believe that in a few short months such a wonderful family could be so unceremoniously dismantled. "I'm sorry" was all I could manage.

I'm not proud to say this, but we got out of there as fast as we could. The warm, wonderful Thanksgiving tradition we had always shared with the Claytons had ended, cold turkey. "That was awful," Trevor said on the drive home.

"I miss Elise," Savannah said. "And Judy." Nobody disagreed.

And then the kids started talking about all the things Judy had done, every year, to make Thanksgiving so special—the food, the decorations, the toast "to family" where we held our glasses aloft. It was sad and unnatural not to have her there. The value she added to their family was tremendous; it wasn't the same without her. When Mitchell decided to separate from his wife, he had clearly not thought through the devastating cost to his family or to himself. He was so hell-bent on pursuing what he thought would be his personal happiness that he had destroyed everything he had worked so hard to build.

"He took Judy for granted," Linda said. "He threw away his family dynasty. There's no coming back from that."

And that's when it hit me how right Linda was. The family dynasty was the heart of everything—home, happiness, financial security and freedom. It was essential: a dynasty that is grown carefully and prudently over many years, first between two partners, then expanding to include kids, relatives and other families. Over the coming months, that idea would percolate, taking on more substance until it eventually became this book.

———

What is a family dynasty? By my definition, a dynasty is not just the people you are related to by blood. It encompasses all the significant relationships in your life. In addition to your parents, siblings and kids, there are the business relationships that enable you to build your fortune. There are the friends and family who act as a support system and network, both personal and professional. Over your lifetime, you will constantly invest capital in other people, whether that capital is money, resources or time. Each of these relationships has a role in building and preserving your family dynasty.

Anybody can have a family, but growing a dynasty requires a special kind of diligence and commitment and results in a solid financial and emotional gain over time. I like to think of a family as the largest asset base you'll ever build. In this book, I urge you to treat your dynasty as a long-term financial asset. Forming a family is in some ways similar to setting up a business. Like any business, your family will have different attributes and assets: some emotional, some financial. Take, for example, the investment you make in your children's education: when you send a son or daughter off to university or trade school, you're strengthening the underpinning of your family's success. If you spend, save and invest wisely, the assets you have today will become even greater assets tomorrow.

The cost of losing these assets is very high. Take Mitchell Clayton, who ran his most important relationships through the shredder, whether he wanted to or not. Mitchell wound up unhappy, with a broken home and a heart-stopping alimony payment. Why? Because he didn't realize the value his wife brought to their family until it was too late. Mitchell's partnership with Judy—in which he'd invested over 30 years of equity—was the most valuable asset in his life, and now he'll never be able to get it back.

But if you make the *right* choices, you can protect and grow your assets. When you reduce debt and protect your personal and business relationships, when you set financial targets and are responsible enough to meet them, you're not only creating success in *your* lifetime—you've just set your kids up for success in the future as well. And if you build a dynasty properly, introducing family values to your children, they will avoid the fate of some young people today who learn only to be entitled bloodsuckers feeding off the family fortune. Your kids will learn that to be part of the dynasty, they have to contribute to it, too.

I'm not saying a family dynasty is all about money. But it takes money to create security, stability and freedom for the important people in your life—yourself, your partner and your kids. The cold hard truth is that too many people think they can build a family out of dreams and good intentions; then they end up living below the poverty line with four kids and not nearly enough resources to live a good life. I'll tell you right now: the road to financial ruin is paved with dreams and good intentions. Your kids don't deserve to be destitute, and neither do you.

In this book, I'll show you how to build and maintain a strong dynasty and how to make sound financial choices that will keep you secure, now and well into the future. I'll show you how to make smart money and life decisions, from choosing a partner who increases your financial and emotional security, to paying off your mortgage and growing your savings, to showing your children how to appreciate the value of both money and family. I'll share tips and strategies to ensure your kids grow up just as money-savvy as you are. We'll even talk about what to do if your relationships, personal and business, are on the rocks; I'll guide you through how to separate your money from your emotions and how to save your assets in times of trouble. By the time you've finished this book, you'll have the building blocks you need to create a life and legacy of wealth, happiness and freedom.

Are you ready to take control and build a solid and rewarding family dynasty? Read on.

Taken in 1987, when Linda, my future wife, and I were still dating. I am all about a long courtship. It helps determine if you are compatible with your partner. Sure, romance matters, but in the long run getting married is as much a business decision as a romantic one. Raising a family is no small undertaking. Choosing a person who shares your life goals is very important.

PART ONE

LOVE

CHAPTER 1

THE DATING GAME

If you've read my previous books, you know my mother, Georgette, was a financial wunderkind. She took over the family clothing business at a young age and, through careful money management and smart investing, was able to amass a small fortune. She survived the premature death of my father, Terry, whose "life of the party" personality disintegrated into serious money problems a few years into their marriage. But when my mother married for the second time, she did things differently. She readjusted her criteria and learned from her mistakes, revamping her entire approach to choosing a life partner. The change came partly out of necessity—this time, she had to think about what was best for her two children, my brother, Shane, and me—and partly out of a desire to build a marriage and a family that would last.

And last it did. Georgette married my stepfather, George, in 1962, and they forged a happy, healthy, secure partnership that continued until my mother's death in 2008. How many people can claim 46 years of wedded bliss? Not many, according to the statistics. A recent study showed more than one-third of marriages end in divorce before the 30th anniversary. That's a lot of broken hearts and a lot of thin wallets.

It doesn't have to be that way. The truth is, a successful marriage is like a pizza pie, and love is only one slice. You can argue that love is an important slice, and I won't disagree with you. But there are other slices, too, slices nobody wants to talk about in our rom-com–saturated world. If you know anything about me, it probably won't surprise you to hear me stress the importance of money above romance.

I'm not saying you should marry a millionaire. When my mother married George, his life savings fit easily into his pocket. He went to the notary's office with my two uncles to obtain a marriage contract, and when the notary asked him about his liquid assets, he answered honestly, "I've got 36 to my name."

"Thirty-six thousand?" the notary asked. "That's great!"

"No," George answered. "Thirty-six *dollars.*"

You might think my mother was crazy, getting hitched to a man with so little to his name. She wasn't. George was a smart investment. A year after they married, he completed his PhD in business from the University of Illinois and obtained a plum position as an advisor and consultant with a United Nations agency. I benefited from a multicultural upbringing because of George's appointments in countries as far-flung as Cambodia, Cyprus, Ethiopia and Tunisia.

Of course, no one has a crystal ball, including my mother. Georgette had no way of knowing with 100 percent certainty that George would turn out to be a smart investment. But she did do some things differently to create financial security for herself and her sons.

First, she did *relationship due diligence*. George and Georgette dated for more than three years before they got married. They had plenty of time to get to know one another and to suss out core compatibilities as well as identify any potential roadblocks. And second, *she went into the relationship with her own money*.

As co-owner of the family clothing business in Montreal, my mother had her own funds. She met George during a brief holiday abroad. Their first date was nothing extravagant: they went dancing with friends and collected seashells in my mother's oversized straw hat. George was a man of modest means; he and Georgette used public transportation, as owning a car was a great luxury in those days. As their relationship progressed, they took long walks by the ocean and frequented ethnic restaurants to soak up the local flavor—but they didn't spend on anything fancy during their courtship. George didn't try to impress my mother with lavish dinners or extravagant gifts he could not afford. Even in those early days, Georgette was vetting her future husband, whether she was aware of it or not—and he was passing the test. Their courtship assured her that they could both be happy even during lean economic times.

The two of them had long conversations about every detail of their proposed partnership, including their goals regarding money, family and quality of life. My mother was adamant that Shane and I get to know George before she married him; if any red flags or serious issues had surfaced, I have no doubt she would have pulled the plug. Fortunately for all of us, George had a natural aptitude as a father and as a provider, which he continues to demonstrate to this day. I now think of George as my father, and indeed, he is (but more on that later).

My mother financed the wedding, a simple yet tasteful affair with about 20 guests. Once George became the breadwinner, he made it abundantly clear that Georgette's money was her own; he had no interest in how much she had or how she spent it. While Terry had been threatened by the fact that my mother had her own funds and accounts, George encouraged her financial independence. My mother had found a life partner who had the same money values and a shared understanding of how financial independence works within a marriage. They weren't idealistic kids drinking the Kool-Aid of romantic love. George and Georgette saw marriage as a contract: two people coming together to build a dynasty, one based on emotional closeness, but one that doesn't exclude financial prudence.

Why am I telling you this story? Because if you want a partnership and dynasty that last, take a cue from my mother. Love, marriage and kids can provide some of the richest rewards in life—but only if you have a strong financial foundation to support them. It's up to you to start building that foundation from your very first date.

━━━━━

Dating is a racket. It's an endless cavalcade of dashed hopes and squandered dollars, yet for some reason, people keep coming back to it. Ever wonder why dating shows are the bread and butter of reality television? People tune in to *The Bachelor* every week hoping the contestants will find "true love." The more tears and breakdowns they encounter along the way, the higher the ratings. Because true love is worth any cost, right?

Wrong. In real life, this approach will send you straight to the poorhouse (and it doesn't seem to be working wonders for reality TV stars, either). The last thing you want is the financial burden of multiple breakups. Your goal is to find a mate and stay with him or her *for your entire life*. I want you to be happy—not just emotionally, but financially. Thank goodness you've found me: I'm here to guide you toward financial happiness. There's a reason this chapter is called "The Dating Game." You have to play to win.

Money Mistake: *You Think Dating Means Spending*
The Fix: *Avoid the Four Common Money Leaks*

When you're dating, you naturally want to put your best foot forward. Who doesn't want to look great and be charming? But the more you puff yourself up into something you're not, the more it's going to cost you later. Keeping your ego nicely stroked is not cheap. It's also not worth it. When you *do* meet the person you're going to spend the rest of your life with, why on earth would you want to start your relationship in debt?

There are four common money leaks in dating, four incidentals that slowly sap away more dollars than you realize: transportation, fancy dinners, expensive clothes and online dating sites.

First: the cost of cars and cabs. Guys, if you think a flashy car is going to be your ticket to getting the ladies, think again. Let me put it to you plainly: *you do not need a flashy car when you're young and penniless.* I remember that one of my friends from university had a 1969 Camaro with baby blue pinstripes and whitewall tires. I'll admit that car was a thing of beauty. My friend spent every weekend waxing it until it shone, and he spent hundreds of dollars each month adding every imaginable bell and whistle.

"Chicks dig Camaros," he said to me, though most of the time his girlfriend was annoyed by how much attention he lavished on that car instead of on her. Then one night he hit a patch of black ice and totaled it. Fortunately, he was fine, but the car wasn't. All that money he spent on it and the car amounted to a hunk of junk.

Maybe you read my second book and know how I feel about cars. You were so inspired you sold your automotive money pit and are now the proud owner of an electric bike. But now you're looking at me, saying, "Uncle Kevin, I can't pick up that pretty girl on an electric bike. I'll just splurge on a cab this one time and shell out $30 (plus tip) for a one-way trip to that classy Yorkville bistro I read about on Yelp."

Guess what? By the end of the night, you're going to spend a minimum of $200 when you could have grilled hamburgers back at your place for under $20.

"But Uncle K," you say, "hamburgers are not the food of love. She won't love me if I don't shell out." Really? Guess what, pal. If spending your money is her main goal, I'm giving you free license to dump her. Now. Cut your losses now. You'll thank me for it later.

Which brings me to money leak number two: fancy dinners. I love a good steak and a nice glass of wine, but when you're dating, it's not just the quality you're paying for, it's the quantity. A meal at a five-star restaurant, with drinks, costs more than $100 *per person*. With gratuity, your dinner bill will probably come to $300. But you're not just going on one date. You are actively vetting potential future mates, which means you may be going out on two, even three dates a week. That $300 can skyrocket to $900 over the course of a single weekend. If your dance card is really full, you're looking at spending close to $4,000 *a month*. Suddenly, your social life costs more than your apartment! Something's got to give.

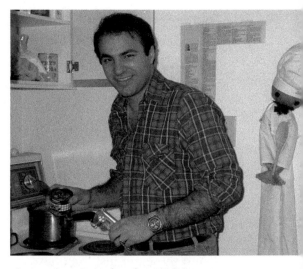

I love cooking. One of my favorite dishes is escargots served in the shell. When I was single, my best strategy was to bring my date over to my place for a romantic dinner where I would start with my escargots and end with my crêpes flambées. It was far less expensive than going to a high-end restaurant, and showing off my culinary skills gave me a competitive advantage. It significantly improved my batting average! My future wife, Linda, took this picture on our second date in 1982.

Then there's the money you spend on clothes. Obviously, you don't want to go on a date wearing pajama bottoms. There's no reason to be slovenly; you want to make a good presentation. But that doesn't mean you need to overinflate your wardrobe with pricey pieces. The key is to carefully select a handful of timeless classics and then mix and match. In my last book, I mentioned the stylish Chanel jacket my mother wore for 20 years. My daughter, Savannah, has put a new twist on the family tradition: she recently bought a great dress for $10. It was too big for her, so she had it altered for $20. She now has a $30 dress that people think is worth $1,000. Talk about the new Georgette! Those are the kind of family values I want to pass from generation to generation.

The fourth and final money leak is bigger than the previous three combined. In recent years, online dating has experienced a meteoric surge in popularity. An estimated 30 to 40 million North Americans now use online dating sites, with more than 1,500 different websites catering to the lonely masses. The industry is worth over $1.5 billion—not at all surprising when you consider that a quarter of all Canadians have tried Internet dating. And those are just the ones being honest about it.

I'm not going to weigh in on the efficacy of online dating or how likely you are to find lasting love with the click of a mouse. That's not my department. The question I want you to ask yourself is: How much of that $1.5 billion is coming out of *your* pocket? And are you getting your money's worth? First, there are the obvious price tags. Average membership on an Internet dating site ranges from $30 to $60 a month—double that at the more "exclusive" sites. Also, keep in mind that online dating enables a higher quantity of dates because of the larger pool of potential partners. I've known people with active profiles on multiple websites who go out with a different person every night of the week, and sometimes more than once a day. The first three money leaks—transportation, fancy dinners, expensive clothes—are still sucking money away, only now it's on a much bigger scale. Spend $300 eight or nine times a week and the costs are staggering. One month will put a $10,800 dent in your wallet—or more likely, your credit card. And more often than not, all of that cash spent doesn't result in any kind of long-lasting relationship; rather, it results in less cash in the wallet and more heartbreak and loneliness.

Then there are the hidden costs. With the rise of online dating has come a parallel rise in online dating scams. Take Teresa, a woman who truly believed she had met her soulmate. Philip claimed to be a humanitarian aid worker currently deployed overseas. They exchanged dozens of emails, and Philip sent Teresa pictures of himself and his young daughter. After several months, the daughter purportedly got sick. Soon Philip was asking Teresa for money, and against her better judgment, she was sending it. By the time she figured out what was going on, she had sent him over $40,000.

I don't have a lot of sympathy for the Teresas of the world. If you are managing your finances the way you should, you're not going to dole out a dollar, never mind 40 grand, to a man you've never met. Teresa paid a high price for not performing due diligence on her partner (more about that in chapter 2). But love, even just the promise of it, is a powerful drug. Teresa thought she'd found it with Philip, and in her mind, that was worth any cost. Problem was, it wasn't love at all. It was extortion. Beware of emotions when it comes to romance, because when logical thinking escapes you, a cash drain isn't too far behind.

Internet dating sites are still largely unregulated, which means they are a minefield of potential scammers and thieves. The Canadian Anti-Fraud Centre estimates Canadians lost at least $17 million to online dating scams in 2012. Remarkably, fewer than 5 percent of fraud cases are reported to authorities, perhaps because victims are ashamed of having been duped or simply because people tend to be tight-lipped about love and money.

Unfortunately, if you're the target of an online dating scam, you're going to lose both.

The number one rule in real estate is "location, location, location," and the number one rule in relationships is "time, time, time." Time is the best litmus test for true love. All told, Teresa had known Philip for only eight months—and I use the term "known" lightly. (In Teresa's case, she made the ultimate mistake of never coming face to face with Philip at all and never getting to know him for real.) Most scammers don't have the patience or the resources to pull off a long con. The longer you know someone, the more layers of deception and posturing get peeled away, until you're finally face to face with the cold hard truth.

Money Mistake: *You've Met Mr. or Ms. Wonderful—Time to Get Married!*
The Fix: *Follow the Three-Year Rule*

My mother had a simple rule: wait three years before marrying someone. She learned this lesson the hard way. Her courtship with my father was brief, and the results were disastrous.

"You need three full years," she always told Shane and me. "One year to fall head over heels, one year for all the potential problems to surface, and one year to decide whether those problems are deal breakers or things you can work through."

If you're lucky enough to find love, in the first year enjoy the jubilation of romance. It may seem in those early months of the relationship that your partner can do no wrong. You are hopped up on hormones and the exhilaration of exploring something (and someone) new. Enjoy the fireworks and butterflies, but avoid making any major life decisions. Don't move in together, don't make any major purchases and don't start planning the wedding. Do pay attention to your partner's spending habits, including how cavalierly they whip out their credit card. And do have important conversations about where you see yourself in the future. Do you want to work full time or stay home with the kids? Do you *want* kids? Now is the time to articulate your long-term objectives and see if your partner's objectives line up with yours. If they don't, cut your losses before someone gets hurt.

In the second year, the luster of new love starts to wear off. That's okay—it means you're seeing who your partner really is, not the idealized version you spent the last year mooning over. When the fireworks fizzle, you'll begin to notice personality idiosyncrasies and prior baggage that may become problematic down the line. Does she spend money she doesn't have on junk food and vacations? Is he still paying off his college loans? Worse: Is he completely ignoring his loans as they continue to accumulate interest? Even if it *seemed* like you were in agreement about saving money and paying down debt, actions speak louder than words. Maybe you are suddenly up-front-and-personal with your partner's issues in a way you never were when you only saw each other once a week. The second year requires greater scrutiny and a more realistic outlook. Your partner isn't perfect, and neither are you. Now is the time to note each other's blemishes.

The third year is when you determine whether you can live with a person's deficiencies and defects. Hopefully, this is still the person you fell in love with, the one who lit the initial fireworks. But here is where relationship due diligence becomes critical. In the third year, it's time to ask some tough financial questions—and carefully weigh the answers. What is your partner's credit rating? If the score is low, you deserve to know why. How much debt do they have? What is their monthly budget? This is also the time to draw up the hypothetical household budget you'd be operating under if you were to get married or live together, and to decide on specific financial roles. Every marriage requires certain day-to-day tasks—keeping track of accounts, paying bills, filing taxes—as well as longer-term responsibilities, such as investments and wealth management. The third year is when you decide who does what. And will that change as your relationship progresses? If your partner has certain money behaviors or inefficiencies that concern you, make an appointment with a financial advisor immediately to get a third-person perspective. Be honest with yourself and with your advisor. Is it the right choice to build a life with this person? If the answer is yes, pass Go and collect $200. If the answer is no, move on. Far better to know you're not compatible now than 10 years down the road, once you've got a marriage, house and kids at stake.

By the way: if it becomes clear for any reason that you're never going to have children with this person, don't bother getting married. You can cohabitate for the rest of your life, but there's no need to enter into a contract. This was one of the most controversial points in my second book, but I stand behind it. A marriage contract sets up the structure and legal protection for your future family. If you're not going to have kids, what's the point?

Right now, you may be thinking, "Whoa, Kevin. I'm not dating seriously—I'm just having fun. What's wrong with that?" I'll tell you what's wrong with that: chances are the fun you're having is blowing a hole through your pocket. And if you're not planning for the future, how will you recognize Mr. or Mrs. Right? Even if you're only in your 20s, you should be actively identifying your goals regarding finances, career, partnership and family. If you want to be happy, you're going to need to find a mate who is in sync with you in each area. And if you want a successful 46-year marriage like my mother's, you're going to have to take this stuff more seriously. Starting now.

EIGHT DATES THAT
WON'T BREAK THE BANK

Dating doesn't have to cost a fortune. Sometimes the best bonding experiences are the ones that cost the least. Here are eight ideas for fun, memorable dates that won't hurt the wallet.

1. **Take a stroll**. It's no coincidence that both walking and dancing played a key role in the early days of George and Georgette's courtship. Moving your body makes you feel good. It's also *free*. When my wife, Linda, and I started dating, we walked everywhere. Exercise boosts your energy level, delivering oxygen and nutrients to your heart, lungs and brain. It also gives couples a chance to talk. Why not take a day hike or bike around town? Linda and I used to rent bicycles to get from A to B—many big cities have wonderful bike paths. We also went skating in the winter. Find a place where you can rent a cheap pair of skates and hit the ice. Bonus: you're getting a jump start on a healthy relationship. Literally.

2. **Explore a museum or an art gallery**. Taking your date to a museum is a great way to stimulate conversation. And I'm not talking about dull dinosaurs; I'm talking about cool modern exhibits on art and music. Last winter, there was a Patti Smith exhibit at the Royal Ontario Museum in Toronto. Linda and I loved it. We'll definitely be checking out the David Bowie exhibit at the Art Gallery of Ontario, too. If you're a member, admission is often free for you and a guest. If you're not, scan an events calendar. Most cities offer free admission on certain days of the month. Bonus: your date will be impressed by your deep cultural appreciation.

3. **Sweat it out.** If you want to turn up the dial on physical activity, move some furniture. It may sound strange, but it's also surprisingly intimate to help a girl move her coffee table or a guy to rearrange his office. Something about it triggers that "nesting" instinct and tests some fundamental personality matches.

   I used to have these huge speakers that weighed way more than Linda did: 300 pounds each. I kept them on the first floor of my house, but one Friday night, I decided I wanted to put them up on the third floor. All my roommates were gone, so it was up to Linda and me. We heaved and pushed and cursed and carried those speakers up three flights of stairs. That was our Friday date night. We did it together and were proud of ourselves when we'd managed the impossible. I still remember collapsing onto the sofa once we were done, Linda and I sitting side by side, listening to music together. Somehow, moving furniture had become an event, a trial we had to work together to get through, and it strengthened the bond between us. Bonus: we didn't have to pay movers.

4. **Board it up.** Have a competitive streak? Pull out a couple of classic board games and challenge your date to a night of Monopoly or Balderdash. Today, many cities have board game cafés, where the cost of a coffee or beer will grant you access to stacks and stacks of games. It's good, cheap fun and you'll earn extra marks for creativity. Bonus: a chance to see whether your date has a competitive streak (which, I'd say, might be a good thing!).

5. **It's just brunch.** By now, you know not to waste money on lavish dinners. So why not go out for brunch or lunch instead? Fancy restaurants are far more affordable in the A.M. than in the P.M.

Some places offer outrageous deals and specials to fill seats during the midday dead zone. Bonus: you'll get to see what your date looks like in the cold hard light of day.

6. **Dinner and a movie—with a twist.** There's something to be said for keeping with tradition; no harm in following a tried-and-true formula. But forgo the $18-per-ticket summer blockbuster and pick up a movie at your local library instead (free if you're a patron). Or download a film online for $2.99 and cuddle up with your honey at home. If you're gifted with culinary prowess, make dinner yourself. Bonus: since you're playing host or hostess, you might get to relax by kicking off more than your shoes.

7. **Find a meetup group.** Meetup.com was started by a couple of guys in New York City in the wake of the September 11 attacks. They wanted to make it easier for people to connect with strangers in their community. Now Meetup is flourishing, with groups and events in hundreds of cities. You can create a profile at no cost and then search for groups by common interests—everything from photography to squash to investing to ikebana. Most events are free. What's great about Meetup is that you are introduced to a group of potential partners who share at least one of your interests. Bonus: by meeting people in a large social setting, you'll alleviate the high pressure (and high cost) of a first date.

8. **Online dating version 2.0.** According to *The Globe and Mail*, Canada is a hotbed for online dating. If you're dead set on keeping up with the trends, nothing I say is going to dissuade you. At the very least, try your luck on some of the free dating sites before doling out hefty membership fees. Sites like Plentyoffish.com, launched in 2003 out of an apartment in British Columbia, are giving the big corporate sites a run for

their money. In Canada, Plenty of Fish (POF) gets twice as many unique visitors as eHarmony each month, and *10 times* as many total visits. POF boasts 55 million members with 50,000 new signups per day. Fifty-five million people isn't just a pool of members—it's an ocean.

CHAPTER 2

CHOOSING A MATE

We all go to school to learn the basics—reading, writing and arithmetic. But no one ever teaches us how to choose a future mate. Seems like a significant gap in the education system, if you ask me. Your mate isn't someone with whom you're going to spend an afternoon or a few sunny weeks of vacation. We're talking about *the rest of your life*. And here's the important part: your mate is going to be the biggest investment you ever make, and if you choose wrong, you're going to pay for it.

I had seen my mother's marriage to my father collapse over money trouble, and I had no desire for a repeat performance. I had also watched Georgette forge a successful partnership with George. By the time I was a teenager, I had committed the Three-Year Rule to memory and knew how to date frugally—more by necessity than by choice, I can now admit. But it wasn't until I was in my late 20s that I met the woman who would become my wife.

In the early days of SoftKey, a software company I launched that became a very lucrative business, I was still working from home—from my basement, to be exact. You might find it hard to believe, but I didn't always sit for hours at a time on the set of *Dragons' Den* or *Shark Tank*. To get my blood pumping, I'd hit the gym at the Toronto Squash Club. Back then, I was in pretty good shape—and there was no waiting around on set for the ever-present camera, which has since added an extra 10 pounds.

When *Shark Tank* became the number one show in its fourth season, the network began to promote it aggressively. Here I am shooting a new title sequence for the show, with a wide range of expensive hardware! These TV shoots take hours: I remember arriving at this facility at noon but not leaving until midnight.

One day, I was resting on the workout equipment when the pretty blonde fitness director came up to me, tapped me on the shoulder and said, "Excuse me, sir. You need to get off the equipment so that other people can use it." Those were my wife's first words to me. Hardly a love ballad, but it was enough to get my attention. I started looking for her whenever I went to the club. I talked with her a little and found out she was still in university, working as a fitness director at the club to support herself. She moved with confidence and purpose, and it wasn't long before I asked her out.

"No, no," she said the first time I asked. "I can't go out with you. I have a boyfriend."

"I don't want to take him out," I said. "I want to take *you* out!"

I was persistent. For months I kept asking, always getting the same response. "Can't. I'm already seeing someone." Then I stopped asking for a few weeks, and—wouldn't you know it—that's when she got a little bit interested.

My roommates and I were throwing a huge party and, unbeknownst to me, Linda got herself on the invite list through one of my friends. We hit it off immediately, just like I knew we would. After that night, Linda and I were an item. The other guy she'd been dating was toast.

Our courtship was very simple. There were no lavish dinners, no decadent vacations, no luxury cruises and weekend shopping trips to Paris. Linda and I were united in a common purpose: to enjoy our time together without worrying about our finances. We spent most of our time with three other couples, and the eight of us watched movies on the third floor of my house; we ordered takeout from Mr. Pong's, the best (and most economical) Chinese food in Toronto. We hosted backyard barbecues—hot dogs, hamburgers, cheap beer and wine. It was nothing fancy. Linda was a student and I was just starting my business. We didn't have a fortune, but we did have fun.

Linda and I dated for six years before we got married. We broke up once in the middle before getting back together a few months later. By the time we finally tied the knot, we had doubled Georgette's Three-Year Rule. We weren't starry-eyed kids rushing full tilt down the aisle. We had tested our relationship, figured out our core compatibilities and made a plan for a partnership that would last. The fact that we are still married 24 years later means we must have done something right.

Money Mistake: *You Don't Know Your Partner*
The Fix: *Perform Relationship Due Diligence*

I would never put my money into a business without doing due diligence first. If I'm interested in something I've seen on *Dragons' Den* or *Shark Tank*, I vet the company thoroughly before I part with a single dime. I've got a whole team of people who review and analyze every financial record, plus anything else deemed material to the investment. Frankly, the majority of deals don't make it past this process alive. When you see a deal pass muster on *Dragons' Den*, only one in three of those deals actually closes. That means two-thirds don't survive due diligence. I'm always amazed by all the lies and deception that surface once we've dug deeply into the financials of companies. I guess people are desperate to make their stories sound impressive, so they sometimes exaggerate, omit facts and flat-out lie the minute the cameras start rolling.

Due diligence keeps people honest. At the very least, it's a

Here I am working the red carpet in Hollywood with the other Sharks at the launch of season five of *Shark Tank*. Like *Dragons' Den* in Canada, few people watched *Shark Tank* in the U.S. for the first three seasons. By the end of the fourth season, it was the number one show in America on Friday nights. I'm particularly proud of its popularity among teens.

process that separates shysters from the honest folk. You should perform due diligence before entering into *any* kind of agreement or transaction—and that includes romantic relationships. If that sounds cold, I want you to wipe the stars out of your eyes. Why *wouldn't* you perform a relationship due diligence on a partner you're intending to spend the rest of your life with? You'd do so if it were a business, so why not for the most important contract of your life? If more people took this advice, the divorce rate in Canada wouldn't still be hovering around 40 percent.

Lucky for you, my goal is to keep you out of that 40th percentile. I want to help you understand that your romantic relationship is a business transaction. Marriage is a contract. It's no different than the deals I make on *Shark Tank* or *Dragons' Den*: both sides commit to working together toward a mutually agreed-upon end. Because I would never invest in a business before performing due diligence, I'm going to suggest you take the same approach.

We have an internal document that we use at O'Leary Ventures: a thorough questionnaire we ask every company to complete. I've modified the checklist so that it's applicable to you and your relationship. I'm not saying you have to slam a Relationship Due Diligence checklist down in front of every person you date—but I'm also not saying that's a bad idea, especially when things get serious. I've been doing this in business for a while now, and believe me when I say the truth will always come out in the end. Better to know it now than suffer the consequences later.

RELATIONSHIP DUE DILIGENCE

The best way to get your partner to fill out a Relationship Due Diligence checklist is to ask outright. Don't soft-shoe around it;

simply explain that you take this relationship seriously and, before you go any further, you need to respectfully ask some financial questions and you'd appreciate your partner's honest replies. If you like, you can offer to fill out a checklist yourself first. Clear off a table and sit down together with all your financial documents—bank statements, tax returns, credit scores, etc. If you want to take the pressure off, do it over a glass of wine. This stuff doesn't have to be a big deal, and some of the answers you may already know; but if your prospective partner has a tantrum, well, that should tell you something. Make it clear to your partner that this process is only going to bring you closer as a couple. Financial intimacy starts here.

Work/Income

What is your occupation?_____

Do you work full time or part time?_____

How many hours per week?_____

What is your monthly income from your job? _____

Do you draw a salary from a business you own? If so, how much?

_____

Please list your employment history, including any businesses that you have started in the past. Include name of company, start date/end date, your role, and the reason for your departure if the business is defunct or if you've opted out of it. _____

_____

_____

_____

_____

_____

Educational Background

Please circle the highest level of education obtained:
Post-Graduate, Graduate, Undergraduate, College/Diploma,
High School

At which educational institutions have you studied? When?

_____

Did you complete your course of study?

_____

Do you have any degrees?

_____

Please specify any professional designations held and the dates
they were granted. _____

_____

Personal Background

Have you struggled with alcoholism or drug addiction?

_____

Have you been in formal treatment for alcoholism or drug
addiction? If so, where? _____
How long was length of treatment? _____
Was treatment ultimately successful? _____
Is there anything else you wish to share about this topic or a related
topic?_____

_____

Criminal History

Have you ever pleaded guilty to, or been found guilty of, a criminal
offense?_____

Are you the subject of any current charge, indictment or proceeding for a criminal offense? _____

If so, please detail the offense charge, location (city, country), date and sentence. _____

_____

Is there anything else you wish to share about this topic or a related topic? _____

_____

Regulatory Investigation

Have you ever been charged with an offense or are you currently the subject of an investigation by any self-regulatory authority, including any securities regulatory authorities? _____

If so, please detail the offense charge, regulatory authority, location (city, country), date and sentence. _____

_____

Is there anything else you wish to share about this topic or a related topic? _____

_____

Personal Debt

Do you own or rent your home? _____

What is your credit rating? _____

List below any monthly debts owed:

Mortgage (if you own) _____

Credit card debt _____

Student loans _____

Personal loans _____

Loans from other businesses that you own _____

Alimony_____

Child support _____

Auto loan _____

Other debt (please list) _____

_____

Please list all credit cards that you have and include amount owed on each:_____

_____

_____

Has your home ever been foreclosed on? If so, when? _____

_____

Have you declared or been petitioned into personal bankruptcy? If so, when? _____

_____

Cash Flow

Is your income covering your expenses on an ongoing basis?

_____

If so, how much are you clearing above your expenses monthly?

_____

If not, how much of a shortfall monthly?

_____

How much do you have in savings?

_____

Do you have an investment portfolio? If so, provide details.

_____

_____

_____

Future Goals

If we were to get married, who would run the home? _____

Who would handle the day-to-day financial tasks—i.e., keeping track of accounts, paying bills, filing taxes? _____

Who would handle the longer-term responsibilities of investing money, acquiring assets and managing wealth?_____

Would our financial roles change over time? _____

Would we rely on two incomes or one?_____

Do you want to have children? How many? _____

Who would teach our children about money? _____

Do you want to own a home? _____

How about a second home? _____

Do you want to own your own business? _____

Where do you see us in five years? What do our finances, family and lifestyle look like?_____

How about in 10 years? _____

Twenty? _____

Thirty? _____

Family History

What is your father's name and occupation? _____

_____

What is your mother's name and occupation?_____

_____

Did you come from a family that was under financial stress?

_____

Do you have any dependents?_____

Are you currently supporting any family members financially?

_____

Professional Assistance

Do you have a lawyer? What is his/her name?

_____

What is the contact information for your lawyer?

_____

Do I have your permission to contact your lawyer? _____
Do you have an accountant? What is his/her name?

_____

What is the contact information for your accountant?

_____

Do I have your permission to contact your accountant? _____
Do you have a financial advisor? What is his/her name?

_____

Do I have your permission to contact your financial advisor? _____
What is the contact information for your financial advisor?

_____

If you think asking your partner to complete a Relationship Due Diligence checklist is an egregious insult, you may want to reconsider tying the knot. All the dirty laundry is going to come out the minute you apply for a loan or buy a house together—and certainly if you adopt a child—so you're going to be filling out questionnaires far more intrusive than this one. It's better to surface any potential issues now, *before* the lawyers get involved.

When Linda and I got married, we had very few assets. I was just getting my business off the ground and I had some stocks I wanted to protect, but that was about it. But even we had many candid discussions about how we wanted to structure our lives. We both knew we wanted a family, and Linda was a self-professed "family girl." She made it clear she wasn't a career woman, and we both knew I was a career man. So we agreed on a clear division of labor that made sense. Now, when we look back on our marriage contract, we laugh. Twenty-four years ago, we walked through our separate apartments and assigned dollar values to everything we owned as part of our financial audit and contract. "This sofa is worth $300. That table is worth $150." We hardly owned anything of value! For us, the marriage contract was a kind of pre-prenup—a way to protect the assets we *would* accumulate in the future. We grew into that contract, in much the same way that we grew into the partnership we have today.

You'll notice the title of this chapter is "choosing a mate," not "choosing a soulmate." It's remarkably pervasive, this idea of a soulmate; sappy love songs and romantic films are sure to keep it in perpetuity. But soulmates aren't discovered, they're grown. You start from nothing and work hard to establish your family dynasty, and the two of you are united against all the challenges you face in your marriage and your life. Overcoming obstacles and accomplishing your goals together—that's the brick and mortar of real partnership, and the key to financial stability and success.

FOUR RED FLAGS TO WATCH OUT FOR IN A MATE

If your Relationship Due Diligence checklist revealed some unsavory truths, it may be time to take your due diligence to the next level. Be especially wary of the red flags that follow.

1. **Long-term liabilities.** Here's a cold hard truth most people prefer to ignore: in most marriages, you're not just marrying your spouse, you are marrying his or her family and everyone in it. Nobody wants to talk about it, but if your partner's parents are broke and need financial help, it's going to be your problem. Who ends up taking care of the elderly when they don't have the money to take care of themselves? Their kids, and sometimes the extended family. If your potential in-laws are on a one-way street to financial destitution, chances are good your potential wife or husband will eventually be asked to start writing checks. Your due diligence can't stop with your partner; you've also got to take a cold hard look at your partner's *family's* ability to support themselves in old age. Are there siblings who are unemployed and likely to become pressure points in the future? It may seem harsh, but doing due diligence now could save you tens of thousands of dollars down the line.

2. **Potential health problems**. Is your partner healthy? Does he or she take care of himself or herself? If not, it's going to cost you later. You've probably heard the old saying, "Go look at the mother." Here's the less patronizing and updated version: "Go look at the parents." If you want to know how your partner will age, take a peek at Mom and Dad. Are they overweight? Diabetic? What medications

are they taking? You'll get a lot of information about who your partner is going to be in the future by studying his stock.

You can also get some definitive answers with a little cash and a spit swab. Angelina Jolie made waves in 2013 by undergoing a preventive double mastectomy after learning she faced an 87 percent risk of breast cancer. She's being lauded far and wide as a true hero of our age. What would you do differently if you knew which diseases you were genetically predisposed to? Thanks to the wonders of modern medicine, you can now know. Organizations like 23andMe offer basic genetic testing: register online, and for only $99, they'll send you a spit kit. They test for more than 40 inherited conditions. I suggest you do this with your partner—make a date out of it. Take a trip to the post office to send in your spit samples, and once you've gotten the results, read them together. It's a relatively cheap and efficient way to understand how your genes impact your health and your wallet. Who knows? It might end up saving your life or your partner's. At very least, it's information you'll want to have moving forward.

I went to business school with a guy who married the love of his life. A few years after graduation, they had beautiful twin girls. The girls were two years old when my friend's wife was diagnosed with liver cancer. She died four months later, one week after her 28th birthday. My friend was devastated. If he had known he had a good chance of losing his wife when she was only 28, would he still have married her? Probably. But he would have been in a much better position to prepare for the future—and I bet he and his wife would have invested in a better life insurance policy and been very careful about saving for the future. As it happened, he was completely unprepared and had to raise two toddlers without a mother and on only one income. The loss of his beloved wife was excruciating, but when compounded with difficult financial situations, it very nearly tore him apart.

3. **Crushing debt**. It could be student loans, medical bills or credit card debt. The thing about debt is there isn't a hierarchy. There's no "good" debt and "bad" debt"—it's all horrific. If your due diligence reveals that your partner has significant debt, proceed with caution. How much debt you are willing to accept is up to you, but a good rule of thumb is that your partner should be paying down the principal every month and be working diligently toward a plan to pay off the debt completely. Draw a line in the sand and agree not to move in together or make wedding plans until he or she is making regular payments and reducing the principal. And each digit of debt should make your blood pressure rise accordingly. Four figures is manageable, if handled proactively. Five figures should give you pause. If it's in six figures, run while you can!

4. **Past bankruptcy or foreclosure.** This one should be obvious, but I'll spell it out for you just in case: *do not get into a relationship with someone who has declared bankruptcy or been foreclosed on.* Could you ask for better proof that your partner is not a good manager of money and assets? A recent survey by TD Ameritrade asked women their top two biggest financial deal breakers in a relationship: 42 percent said bankruptcy and 32 percent said foreclosure. Ladies, I'm impressed. Good answers! Bankruptcy remains on a credit report for up to 10 years and foreclosure for seven, which may seriously impact your partner's ability to get hired or be approved for a car loan or home mortgage in the future. There is some baggage you can live with, but if your partner is toting around a bankruptcy or foreclosure, kick him or her to the curb!

CHAPTER 3

THE FIVE LANGUAGES OF MONEY

The Guardian recently published the results of a fascinating survey. University students were put into pairs and recorded during four-minute speed dates. To the naked ear, every conversation sounded more or less the same. The students followed well-trod topics, from "What are you studying?" to "Where are you from?" But a deeper textual analysis revealed stark differences from conversation to conversation—and remarkable similarities, too. The pairs were scored on "language style matching," and the ones whose matching scores were above average were almost *four times as likely* to pursue future contact than the pairs with dissimilar language styles. New proof for what we've known all along: if you and your chosen mate communicate well, it's a good predictor of a successful relationship.

But there's another predictor that is just as important, if not more so. I'm no linguist, but there's one language in which both you and your partner must be fluent if you want your relationship to work: money.

THE FIVE MONEY LANGUAGES
There are five money languages that people speak, and four of them are problematic. Below I've outlined the "mother tongues" of financial literacy. These are the five ways people spend, save and steal money—and the attendant costs you're likely to incur depending on the fluency of who you marry.

1. The Mooch
The mooch is someone who won't pay for anything. You know the type—he's the one who suggests you go out to eat with a bunch of friends, then claims he forgot his wallet and asks if you can spot him (and never pays you back). Or she ducks out of paying her fair share when it's time to split the bill, claiming the service was poor so she's not adding a tip—and, oh look, it seems she's never heard of tax being added to a bill.

Some mooches come from backgrounds where there was never enough. Never enough money, never enough resources, never enough time. They're stuck in a Depression-era mentality, governed by the economics of scarcity, and if you let them, they will suck you down into the same black hole.

At some point, the mooch will try to borrow money from you, maybe even on the first date. Don't think you're special. The mooch is no stranger to loans from friends and family. Your due diligence may in fact reveal that she has been disenfranchised from her family because she constantly borrowed money from her parents or siblings until the family had no choice but to cut her off. If you marry this person, you, too, will get ostracized from his or her family. That's something you should know up front. Don't say I didn't warn you.

2. The Spendaholic

The spendaholic is someone who tries to buy friendship. We all know who these people are: they're the ones always offering to pay for everybody, trying desperately to appear popular and successful. Don't be fooled. This is a disease masquerading as generosity. Spendaholics are the people who, if they don't get their spending in check, end up in Debtors Anonymous. They almost always have personal debt, which they often hide or minimize, and most of the time it's on their credit cards. According to Equifax Canada, our country's total credit card debt was $76.4 billion at the end of 2012—and a good percentage of that is owed by the spendaholics.

You don't want to be with someone who's got credit card debt. The system is guaranteed to turn your daily existence into a living hell. Here's how life as you know it deteriorates: you miss the first credit card bill, and nothing happens. You're generally given almost 90 days of grace. But that's the tipping point. If the credit card company still hasn't received payment, they send it off to collections. The first thing that collapses is your credit rating. There is an immediate and explosive change in your credit rating that is visible online to anyone with a few bucks to spend. Today, all kinds of people can see your credit rating who couldn't see it before—including your employers. No companies will admit they use the system to check on their employees, but trust me, they do.

Let's say a year or two passes and you still haven't paid off your credit card. Now they start to garnish your paychecks. They are completely within their rights to do this. It's legal. Everywhere you turn, there's wage garnishment, and there's nothing you can do about it.

The third and final step is taken when the collection agencies hire people to hound you. If you've let things get this bad, you're probably also defaulting on your car loan or your mortgage. So now it's a competition between the guy the dealership sent to collect on the car loan (because they'd rather get paid than repossess the car), the guy the bank sent to collect on the mortgage (because they'd rather get paid than take your home) and the guy from credit card collections. You've got three people hounding you relentlessly by phone and email. Sometimes they even come to your front door. These are big agencies, so they're not going to give up. They can—and will—chase you for *years*.

"But Kevin," you say, "my partner isn't a spendaholic. Yes, he's in debt . . . but there were forces beyond his control." Maybe your boyfriend fell on hard times or your girlfriend decided to go back to school for an MFA. Unfortunately, the hows and whys don't matter once a person is deep in debt. In our society, the inability to manage money is most often a character flaw and not a result of a terrible tragedy. Debt is where money becomes your enemy. Money is your most trusted friend, but it always has a sinister element to it, waiting to turn on you. It only takes a momentary lapse—a vacation you couldn't really afford, a medical disaster that strikes when you have no Catastrophe Cash Fund to fall back on—for your money to turn.

The Relationship Due Diligence checklist is the perfect way

to expose a spendaholic. Pay special attention to your prospective partner's credit score. Chances are their credit rating has taken a hit—probably many hits—from years of reckless spending. If your partner has an abysmal score, move on. You can't afford to get involved with someone whose spending is out of control.

3. The Loafer

In the loafer's mind, he's living the good life. He may be an over-aged trustafarian who has always been able to count on Mommy and Daddy to pay the bills, or perhaps he simply has a low stand-ard of living and lacks ambition to aim for more. On the Relationship Due Diligence checklist, there's a high probability he put down his occupation as "artist" or "freelance consultant." I'm not knocking true artists and freelancers, those who actually are financially independent thanks to their talents, but the loafer often masquerades as such without actually pulling it off. He is chronically unemployed, though he claims to be "between jobs." More likely is that he's been perpetually fired because he lacks the motivation to show up and make an effort.

The loafer has never really had to worry about money, so he doesn't understand the importance of working for it. He also doesn't care much about saving it, because past experience has affirmed his life philosophy: when he needs it, it will come. And guess what: those declarations of love he keeps whispering to you? Those are because you're the most beautiful and curvaceous dollar sign he's ever seen.

If you marry a loafer, be prepared to pay all the bills and do all the work for two (or more if you have kids)—for the rest of your married life. If you have financial goals, you're going to be on

Taking a "disco nap" after a late night out in New Orleans with friends. By March 1999, The Learning Company was the largest educational software company in the world. Our sales were closing in on the billion-dollar mark that year and there were several companies interested in buying us. I was constantly on the road with investors and bankers. It was during this period that I developed the ability to take twenty-minute naps anywhere and anytime. No matter how crazy my schedule gets, I still use my power naps to keep going.

your own in attaining them. If you try to have a candid discussion about money, he or she will accuse you of being too uptight or not understanding his or her barriers. And when he brings home that new flat-screen TV? You're the one who'll be paying for it.

4. The Thief
The previous three money languages are rife with problems, but the thief trumps them all. You don't want to marry somebody who steals money outright or who is always bamboozling people out of what is rightfully theirs. The best thieves are wolves in

Armani suits. On the outside, they look like wealthy business-men; on the inside, they're swindlers.

Here's the problem with marrying a thief: you become ostra-cized, not only from your family and your partner's family, but from society. You have a broader group of people who don't want anything to do with you or with your spouse. I know a music pro-moter, a very powerful man, who has ripped people off so many times, he's burned every bridge he ever crossed. He's very wealthy now, but it no longer matters; he's lost all social and business con-nection, which will stunt his future. No one wants to see him any-more, and unfortunately, that means they don't want to see his wife, either. She's a lovely and honest woman, and rightly or wrongly, she is guilty by association. As if it weren't enough to lose her family, friends and community, she's also lost her reputation and good name—all because her husband turned out to be a thief.

5. The Meanie

Sounds bad, doesn't it? But it's not! Finally, here is a money lan-guage I can wholeheartedly endorse. The meanie is a balanced spender who lives within her *means*. She has a healthy approach to saving and investing money, and she knows how to set a budget and stick to it. The meanie says, "Look, there are plenty of things I want and can't afford. But until I can afford them, I'm just going to have to live without them." She makes an ideal partner because she's willing to defer financial gratification, even if it requires scrimping and saving during the early years of marriage. My mother was a meanie who lived by three simple rules: *Don't spend too much. Mostly save. Always invest.* As it turns out, meanies aren't mean at all!

You can see where this is going. The best relationships are the ones between a meanie and a meanie. I don't care who you are, where you're from, or whether you're interested in men, women or goats. What matters is that you speak the same money language as the person you choose to build a life with. And if you're serious about building a financial dynasty, there is only one language that's going to get you where you want to go. Meanies of the world, unite!

Money Mistake: *Your Partner Doesn't Speak Your Money Language*
The Fix: *Find Someone Who Does*

Even if your partner is not a mooch, spendaholic, loafer or thief, he or she may speak a foreign money language. Sometimes you will encounter "translation difficulties" of a different sort.

A few years ago, I was doing a speaking engagement at Ryerson University, and during the Q&A after the lecture, a young man raised his hand. He was a good-looking kid, though he seemed very troubled. He had dark circles under his eyes.

He told me he'd really enjoyed my talk. "I'm hoping you can help me out with something," he said, and when I asked him what was up, he told me his story.

This kid was running a financial services software company out of his dorm room and doing $4 million in sales. If you know my business history, you'll understand why I pricked up my ears immediately. He was both exhausted and exhilarated—a combination I knew well. His business was already extremely successful and he hadn't even graduated yet. But he knew it had tremendous potential, so he was working on it day and night. I congratulated him for what sounded like some really great work, work that was going to pay off well in the future. But what was the problem?

The problem was that he had been dating a girl for four years and they had recently gotten engaged. Earlier that week, his girlfriend had stood in front of him and drawn a line in the sand. "I can't take this anymore," she said. "We don't spend any time together. I don't even see you on weekends. I'm supposedly engaged, but I'm alone all the time. It's got to change or I'm leaving you."

This 22-year-old guy looked at me, terrified. "Tell me, Kevin," he said. "What should I do?"

I asked if he wanted my honest answer, and he said yes.

"Which one's easier to replace?" I asked. "The business you are growing into an empire, or this girlfriend?"

He didn't answer. I proceeded to make my case.

"If you're financially successful, you're going to have a lot of women interested in you. And it certainly sounds like you're going to be successful. I know you've been with this girl for the last four years, but it doesn't sound like she's ready to take the journey that you have to take when you're an entrepreneur who is building his business. She doesn't want to be part of that—she wants you to give it up for her. But what you are building with your company is unique. It's a once-in-a-lifetime opportunity that very few people get. I'm recommending that you don't blow it. Right now, that means your business needs you 24/7. Your girlfriend will either get on board or somebody else will."

A wave of chatter broke out in the audience, and I could tell not everyone agreed with me. I decided this was a great way to stimulate a group discussion. So I put the question to them: What do you think he should do?

The students went nuts. One young woman said, "Mr. O'Leary, you're an animal! Why does it have to be a choice between love and money?" I reminded her that I wasn't the one who said it had to be a choice; the guy's girlfriend had set the terms.

We didn't break that class for 45 minutes. In the end, I put it to a vote. Should the student stay with his business or stay with his girlfriend? The class voted with me. Pragmatism won.

I've got nothing against this girlfriend; I actually respect her. But she simply wasn't the right partner for him at that point in time. If they *had* married and the business had continued to be successful, if she had been willing to give him maybe five more years, they might have enjoyed a very comfortable, happy future together. But she wasn't willing to wait, and he wasn't willing to lose momentum on a really good thing. They obviously weren't right for each other, because they weren't speaking the same money language.

At its peak, The Learning Company was selling educational software in over 40 countries and was still growing. I was always on the road. It was a difficult time for my family as I missed many unique moments in my children's lives. Being an entrepreneur requires sacrifice; you have to remember why you are doing it when you are sitting in a hotel room thousands of miles away from home. Also, if you are going to live an unbalanced life and want a family, you better marry someone who can run the family in your absence.

QUIZ: DO YOU SPEAK THE SAME MONEY LANGUAGE AS YOUR MATE?

How can you tell if you're dating a mooch, a spendaholic, a loafer or a thief? What's it like to build a life with a fellow meanie instead? As a part of your relationship due diligence, take the following quiz. This is for your eyes only, so be truthful—even if you don't always like your answers. The more cold hard truth you can unearth at this stage of the game, the more heartbreak you'll spare yourself in the future.

1. At a romantic dinner for two, your partner:
   a) Reaches for his wallet during dessert and comes up empty-handed, then asks sheepishly if you can cover it "just this once." It's the third time he's asked this month. To make matters worse, he tells the server his steak was undercooked and demands to see the manager for a refund—even though he's already eaten half of it.
   b) Orders the most expensive bottle of wine in the restaurant. He insists that you get an appetizer *and* dessert, even though you're not that hungry, and orders you a tawny port after the meal, even though you'd rather not drink. Per usual, he insists on paying for everything—with his credit card.
   c) Wears sandals and surfer shorts. He spends most of the meal talking about his budding career as an artist—never mind that he isn't actually making any art or selling any of it. When you ask him about the job interviews he mentioned earlier, he shrugs off the question, telling you for the 15th time, "I can't go corporate. It's just not part of my vision."
   d) Sees an old school acquaintance and tries to engage him/her in conversation. But the old friend isn't exactly friendly. You get

the sense that he/she doesn't look kindly on your partner and looks at you with an expression that says, "Cut your losses, fast." When you try to ask the acquaintance about your date, your date interrupts the conversation and sends the friend on his way.

e) Engages you in a candid conversation about what kind of food you'd like to eat and where you'd like to go. Together, you agree upon a budget for the evening, and that helps you narrow down your choice of restaurant. Ultimately, you decide to have a glass of wine and shrimp cocktail at an outdoor bistro before heading back to his place, where he treats you to a simple yet satisfying meal of grilled fish and Spanish rice. And the meal is so good, and everything so relaxed, that it's a great evening for both of you.

2. **When you meet your partner's family for the first time, you wonder:**

a) Why they seem so guarded. They eat very little, and when the meal is over, they don't offer to pick up the tab. Several times, your partner starts to ask them a question and they bristle, as if they are expecting the worst.

b) They treat you both to a fancy four-course meal, no holds barred. You appreciate the generosity, but you recognize the behavior— you've seen your partner make similarly lavish purchases he can't really afford. Aren't his parents retired high school teachers? From the way they're throwing around their credit card, you'd think they were plastic surgeons.

c) How it is possible for parents to so blatantly spoil their adult child. Are they even aware that their son is, in fact, grown up? They coddle and dote on him as if he were still in kindergarten. They worry he isn't resting enough (but he sleeps all day long!)

and they seem convinced he's the next Warhol. By the time you see your partner's father slip him a couple $100 bills and say, "Keep on keepin' on, kiddo," you're seeing a future where he paints soup cans and you exist on them.

d) Whether they in fact exist, because you haven't actually met them. Your partner has left them repeated messages, saying he wants to introduce the three of you. But they won't return his calls. You can't help but wonder what he did to deserve the cold hard shoulder from his own flesh and blood.

e) Why you haven't known them all your life. You've never met two nicer people, and they seem to have a very healthy relationship with their son. He's affectionate with them but not dependent, and the conversation flows freely, topics ranging from retirement planning to this year's hockey lineup. His parents' home is tasteful without being ostentatious, and it's clear where he got his good money sense.

3. **You're planning your first vacation together. Your partner:**
   a) Leaves all the organizing to you. He says it's not his strength, and that's true, but you suspect the real reason is that he's hoping you will pay for the plane fare and hotel reservations.
   b) Plans the most extravagant vacation you've ever heard of, barring celebrity weddings. A luxurious condo on the Kona Coast, five-course dinners every night—even a private masseuse. When you suggest a more frugal approach, he balks. "You deserve to be pampered," he says, but you're pretty sure it's his ego that's getting the pampering.
   c) Asks if you're cool going camping because he's got a pup tent and some firewood. You're actually up for the adventure—until

he forgets to bring any food. You end up with your sleeping bag in the car, too hungry and annoyed to sleep.

d) Suddenly has a large chunk of change and presents you with a plane ticket to Switzerland . . . for *tonight*. When you tell him you need more time, he panics. He seems strangely anxious to get out of the country.

e) Opens a dialogue about cool vacation ideas. Together you come up with the perfect plan: you'll drive a little ways out of the city, where your mutual friends have given you free use of their cottage while they're away for the weekend. You spend two glorious days lazily soaking up sun and getting to know each other better. The best part: you cook all of your meals, which not only gives you bonding time in the kitchen, it means your romantic getaway costs nothing more than a tank of gas and some groceries.

If you primarily answered a), you may be dating a mooch. Your partner treats you like a bank—except that, unlike a bank, money will only trickle out and never in. Time to play hardball and redefine the boundaries of your relationship. Even a bank can renegotiate terms.

If you primarily answered b), you may be dating a spendaholic. Tying your fate to this person is on par with a slow march to debtors' prison. Do not move forward unless you see *serious* improvement with regard to your partner's spending habits, and unless you are 100 percent sure he or she is paying down debt.

If you primarily answered c), you may be dating a loafer. Your partner is still suckling financially from the parental teat. If he or she won't grow up, find someone who will. You deserve better than an over-grown toddler.

If you primarily answered d), you may be dating a thief. Unfortunately, a good thief is notoriously good at defrauding people without being detected. Trust your instincts here. Most of us can tell when something is wrong; it's only when we ignore our instincts that we get into trouble.

If you primarily answered primarily e), congratulations. Looks like you've found a fellow meanie. You're headed in the right direction, toward a life filled with financial happiness and well-deserved success.

This quiz presents some worst-case scenarios, but these are realities for many people. If your partner shows signs of fluency in one of the first four money languages, talk with him or her about it. Voice your fears and concerns. If your partner clearly has no interest in learning to speak meanie, walk away. You're not doing yourself any favors by staying with someone who is spiraling toward a future of financial ruin. You deserve better. And as I said to that Ryerson student, better is out there. You just have to find it—and put a ring on it.

George married my mother, Georgette, on June 30, 1962. I was only eight years old at the time and had no idea what a profound impact my stepfather would have on my life years later. He is still a major influence to this day.

PART TWO

MARRIAGE

CHAPTER 4

ARRANGED MARRIAGE:
WHY IT CAN SOMETIMES WORK

From ancient tribal unions to marriage in the 21st century, society has been figuring out partnership for thousands of years. As long as people have been living, eating, trading, fighting and procreating, a union between individuals has existed in one form or another. The fact that the human race lives on in perpetuity is solid proof. But the love marriage—the marriage that stems from those initial feelings of adulation and infatuation and all too often the blatant disregards common sense—is relatively new.

A long time ago, in a galaxy not so far away, marriage was a way of shoring up important alliances and expanding the family labor force. If you wanted to stay warm and ward off predators, two was better than one, and a whole tribe was better than two. It made sense to have 19 kids because you knew eight were going to die, and the rest were going to be in the fields pulling up root vegetables for dinner. The more children you had, the better your chances of keeping the family alive and robust. Compare that to today, when kids are often parasitic creatures taking refuge in their parents' basements well into their adult years.

Archaeologists have found evidence of formal marriage contracts dating back 4,000 years. Marriage from the beginning was strategic, a way of preserving power, procuring land and producing heirs. Among the common folk, parents and relatives arranged matches to strengthen family ties, while kings and emperors married off their daughters to forge political alliances. Marriage was a union between two people that symbolized a much larger union between two families, tribes or nations. Children often had little say in choosing a mate, daughters especially. In China, there were even "ghost marriages," where living girls were conjoined to deceased men as a goodwill gesture between clans. Being married to a corpse from a good family provided not only financial stability but a good deal of independence. These "widows" were treated respectfully as married woman while enjoying the freedom to pursue their own interests. In other words, they maintained their wealth and reputation, but they didn't have to cook dumplings for their husband or pick up his dirty socks. It was a win-win.

For our ancestors, marriage was never about love or romance or sexual desire. It was about money, property and preserving the family lineage. This led to some rather strange practices among friends. Long before *Wife Swap* was a popular TV show, the ancient Romans were practicing their own version of a marriage exchange. Take Cato, a powerful statesman who was looking for ways to strengthen ties with Hortensius, a well-known Roman orator. Hortensius was a wealthy man and a lover of good wine—an all-around decent guy. But his one regret in life was that he didn't have an heir. So Hortensius proposed that he marry Cato's daughter. Cato wanted to get in good with the orator, but marrying his 20-year-old daughter to his 60-year-old friend was a bit much. Instead, Cato agreed to divorce Marcia, his own wife, to make her legally available. Hortensius liked the idea; he swept in, married Marcia and promptly got her pregnant, which gave him the heir he'd always wanted. In case you think Marcia got the short end of the stick, rest assured she made a tidy profit from this arrangement. When Hortensius died six years later, she inherited most of his considerable wealth, which included multiple villas and a handful of fish ponds. One year later, Marcia and her children moved back into Cato's household, where it is widely believed Cato remarried her. Now, I'm not calling Marcia a gold digger, but it's clear she did pretty well for herself and her kids.

Historically speaking, marriage has always been a practical affair. So when did love start to win over practicality and financial prudence? Who's responsible for the shift to foolishness? For that, we have the Victorians to thank. In the late 1800s, people fell madly in love with the notion of romantic love. Love matches gained cultural currency, and around the turn of the 20th century, mutual attraction became a part of the equation for the first time in history. Young people shocked their parents by refusing to marry the Mr. or Ms. Wonderful to whom they were betrothed, running off instead to elope with Mr. or Ms. Morally Questionable and Officially Bankrupt.

Take the case of Alfred Gilbert, an English sculptor during the late 19th century. At 22, Alfred defied his parents and eloped to Paris with his cousin Alice, the so-called love of his life. It didn't end well. In under a decade, bankruptcy forced Alfred to flee the country, leaving Alice alone with their five children. She left him in 1904 and spent the rest of her life in a mental hospital. No storybook ending there. And maybe even a sign of things to come.

Which brings us to the present. By the time the 20th century rolled around, love matches in the Western world were fast becoming the norm. Marriage moved out of the realm of arranged social contracts and into the realm of romance and sexual desire. You know what else skyrocketed around the same time? The divorce rate.

It's no coincidence. Numerous studies have shown that, in every single society around the globe, as soon as a culture that is widely supportive of arranged marriage is replaced by a culture where individuals choose their own mates, divorce rates start to climb. It's happening right now in China, where the national divorce rate is steadily escalating. An estimated 2.87 million Chinese marriages ended in 2012. That's only 2.2 percent, but just 30 years ago the nation's divorce rate was *.04 percent*. That means out of 10,000 marriages in China, only four failed in 1985. Today, 220 of every 10,000 couples will split.

Why is China experiencing this spike? One reason is that the country has recently introduced new (and simpler) divorce policies, making divorce a possibility whereas in the past it might not have been. But divorces aren't the only business on the rise: young people are adopting new ways of dating and mating that are gradually chipping away at centuries of tradition. The Chinese online dating industry, for example, has really taken off; it is expected to break 2 billion renminbi ($342 million) in total annual revenue by 2014. Goodbye, matchmakers; hello, one-night stands,

If you're like most people I've met in North America, the idea of arranged marriage makes you queasy. "I don't want to be coerced into marrying someone I'm not crazy about. I want to fall madly in love, Uncle Kevin," you whine whenever I bring up the topic. "Of course I'm not proposing forced marriage," I tell you. "That's barbaric. Always was, always will be." Then you say, "Love. Attraction. Romance. That's the way it's supposed to work." Is it? Listen closely: you are a product of your culture. If you lived at any other point in history—and if you lived in a more traditional culture, many of which are alive and well today—you wouldn't be trolling the Internet or going to bars to find a mate. You'd be thanking your lucky stars you had Mom, Grandma or Auntie to find you a partner who was worth your while instead of you, all hopped up on hormones, making stupid decisions that will cost you for the rest of your life. We're talking about the person with whom you're going to share the rest of your life. You can't afford to screw that up.

I'm not going to say that I think arranged marriages are the only way to go. They're not. I'm just saying that at least when an entire family is vetting your potential partner, there's a better chance that a tragic oversight isn't made. Love, as we all know, is blind, but Mom, Grandma and Auntie have six scrutinizing eyes between them, and they have very good reasons not to let a loser or a leech into the family.

I'm going to go out on a limb here and say that I think arranged marriage can often work. I'm not talking about forced marriage, where one or both partners are unduly or totally coerced. I'm talking about consenting adults who've met through familial arrangements where the best interests of all parties factor into the partnership. It may sound crazy, but often your parents and relatives are the people who are best equipped to help you make this all-important decision. "Hold it right there, Mr. Wonderful," you say. "Arranged marriage is politically incorrect. It's a throwback to a time of barbarians." At which point I'd suggest you look at the statistics. Canada's national divorce rate is 40 percent. The average global divorce rate of arranged marriages is 4 percent. All I'm suggesting here is that it's possible that the divorce rate in arranged marriages is lower because those entering into that agreement have entered with awareness and due diligence.

Why should this matter to you? Why is Uncle Kevin suddenly hell-bent on matchmaking? I'm not. I'll leave that to Auntie. But I am interested in helping you make and keep your money, and *there is no greater threat to your family dynasty than divorce*. If you want to get married, it should be your topmost priority to *stay* married. I don't care who you are: the financial damage (not to mention emotional damage) you will incur from a divorce is colossal.

We like to think of ourselves as advanced and savvy, a far cry from our forebears. So

Linda and I in August 2006 at a friend's wedding in Nassau, Bahamas. I was coming out of a three-year retirement and just starting to dabble in a new hobby: television. Life is full of serendipity. You never know what will be just around the corner.

how, with all our education, our so-called experts and our libraries full of self-help books on healthy relationships, are we failing at marriage? Is it possible that when we try to find a partner in a vacuum, stripped out of any larger social context and without the involvement of our families, we are *doing it wrong?*

Not only is it possible, it's true. I'm going to let you in on a little secret: the main reason a marriage breaks up is not infidelity; with hard work, forgiveness and reprioritizing, that can be survived. The real threat to marriage is poor money management or a lack of funds. Not having enough of it, not agreeing on how to manage it, spending too much, saving too little—it's almost always about money. *You want a marriage that will last? Then you had better make sure your partner speaks the same money language.* You had better make sure you have money at the beginning of your marriage, and—this part is non-negotiable—that you have a good deal more of it by the end. One divorce can destroy everything you've built, costing you hundreds of thousands of dollars, if not millions. It is absolutely essential that your partnership run smoothly right out of the gate.

But maybe you're one of the idealistic lovebirds who think they can have it all. You want a storybook romance, but you're also smart with your money and have no intention of making a stupid decision that you'll be paying for for the rest of your life. You're determined not to let your parents meddle in your love life, because you're convinced you are fully capable of finding a sizzling romantic partner with whom you can *also* build a sizable financial dynasty. As far as you're concerned, that's what marriage *is.* "Uncle Kevin," you cry, "I don't care if she's poor; I love her!" Fine. Be a sap, if you must. But find someone who *will* participate in your financial future, and enlist them in every step of the process. If you are missing the money piece, you are making a huge mistake—and you need help. Lucky for you, Uncle Kevin is here.

Money Mistake: *You're Missing the Money Piece of Finding a Mate*
The Fix: *Outsource It*

In many cultures, the matchmaker has always been a highly respected member of the community. In Japan, the *nakodo* acts as a go-between, and in China people pay tribute to Nu Gua, the goddess of matchmakers. Matchmaking has a long, illustrious history, and I'm not the first to suggest that they kind of had it right. Traditionally, matchmakers work alongside the parents and relatives on both sides to ensure a strong, lasting union. As your matchmaker, I'm going to dispense some invaluable money advice, but I'm also going to suggest that if you trust your family, you enlist their help—after all, these are the people who know you best.

Remember how I told you to make the Relationship Due Diligence checklist a mandatory part of dating? Now you don't have to, because your mother's going to do it for you! In an arranged marriage, your family and the matchmaker take care of the due diligence, and they do it long before you're even involved. They're going to get the dirt on your partner's family background, spending habits and financial history. Connecting two families can be very powerful, so they have every reason to take their time and do a thorough check. They are looking for fundamental compatibility at every level. It's their job to find any red flags or potential deal breakers. What assets will be brought into the marriage? Is there debt? Are there long-term liabilities? Will this person be a good provider? Will he or she create stability in the home? Will he or she be a good parent?

It goes both ways, of course. Just as the people on your side are vetting your potential mate, you, too, are being vetted. Your mother or aunt is working with her counterpart on the other side, and together they're taking a long, hard look at what each family will bring to this marriage and why they should or shouldn't endorse it. As a result, you're going to have a formidable infrastructure supporting you as you move forward in this relationship. That's unique. With a love match, you take on every bit of risk yourself. But with arranged marriage, someone else absorbs the risk for you. You'd be a fool not to take advantage of a system that has proven successful for thousands of years.

Perhaps this is why arranged marriage is making a comeback in many cultures. It isn't just the Orthodox Jewish community where matchmakers are thriving. Groups ranging from Southeast Asians to evangelical Christians have begun to adopt the practice. A recent article in the *New York Times* chronicled three American couples who had all been brought together by their families (and one matchmaking service); today, all three are happily married. These men and women were pleasantly surprised to discover they had fallen in love with their partners over time instead of overnight.

At the end of the day, is matchmaking really all that different from your friend at work telling you she knows the perfect girl for you, and then the perfect girl becoming your perfect wife? If your parents are doing their job, they're not going to pick someone you detest; they're going to choose someone you would naturally fall in love with over time. They are seeking someone who will be a good match for you, a compatible partner who will *also* provide a lifetime of financial security. This is why modern matchmakers can charge a pretty penny (one upscale matchmaking service charges clients between $50,000 and $500,000 to find the partner of their dreams). They've got access to a prescreened dating pool. Online matchmaking sites profess to do the same thing, so people spend massive amounts of money to have a bunch of virtual matchmakers find them a match. My question is: Why the hell aren't you using Auntie instead? She's way better at this, and she certainly knows you better than Match.com.

I'm never going to convince you that love has no place in a marriage. If I did, I'd be a hypocrite: I certainly married Linda for love, and we found each other by chance, not through family. But regardless of how you find a mate, money matters. And arranged marriage is a time-tested approach that takes money into account, so it shouldn't be dismissed summarily. It has worked so well for so long. Aren't you at least a little bit curious to see if it could work for you?

FIVE FACTORS
ANY GOOD MATCHMAKER
LOOKS FOR

Whether or not you solicit the help of your family, it's a good idea to start vetting potential mates like a matchmaker would. The key is to not lose objectivity and to assess the match based on predetermined criteria. I don't care how great your partner makes you feel—there are certain factors that may be working against your chances for success without your knowledge. Here are five factors to consider carefully before marrying.

1. **Homogamy.** That's a fancy word for what the dictionary calls "mating of like with like." Over the years, surveys have shown that a marriage between people from similar sociological backgrounds is more likely to last than a marriage between people from dissimilar backgrounds. People who share similar values, norms and beliefs are believed to have an easier time adjusting to one another. That adjustment is what creates harmony in a marriage, whereas heterogamy can increase the chances of discord and unhappiness. Does this mean you should automatically nix a partner who comes from a different background? Of course not. But you should be aware that you and your mate may face a greater number of challenges and difficulties than your homogamous friends. Keep in mind that marital counseling is expensive, and every hour you spend on your therapist's couch working through these issues adds up.

2. **Health.** Research has shown that couples who exercise together enjoy lower stress levels and greater happiness. Staying active will

improve the intimacy in your relationship, giving you a much better shot of staying together. Linda and I met at a fitness center, and going to the gym is still a big part of our lifestyle today. But you don't have to pay pricey membership fees to stay in shape. Take a jog with your partner or even just a walk. Dust off the bicycles from your garage and cruise the neighborhood. There are dozens of ways to exercise without spending a penny. The couple that sweats together stays together.

3. **Social Tendencies.** An ironic consequence of our cyber-connected world is that couples today are more isolated from their communities than ever before. Instead of thriving among a rich network of friends and family, we tend to disengage. We come home from work and veg out to the TV or lose ourselves in our iPads. But studies have shown that couples do best when they engage in the larger community, be it through clubs, service organizations or religious groups. If your mate is a recluse, you may be headed for trouble. Look for someone who has roots—preferably deep ones. And find ways to engage in your community without it breaking the bank. Linda and I have always loved having people over for dinner. It's something we both enjoy—entertaining guests. Another community we're a part of is our local gym. After cooking big meals for our friends and family, we need the exercise!

4. **Education.** This one's a big one: the better educated you are, the better off your marriage will be. And to take it a step further, the better educated a *woman* is, the better the chances of her marriage surviving. Gone are the days when a wife would drop out of school to work full time and put her husband through medical or business school. I encourage *both* partners to work to subsidize their education, even delaying marriage if need be. And by "education,"

I don't just mean university—I'm counting trade and vocational training, too. In these volatile times, broad skills and having two earners with different backgrounds can mean doubling the chance of employability.

5. **Money.** Here's where the average matchmaker could learn a thing or two from me. I'm no psychiatrist, but I do understand money. ~~I understand how having it creates joy and stability in~~ a relationship—and how the lack of it can drive a wedge between even the closest couples. If you and your partner don't speak the same money language, you're destined for financial ruin. If you go into marriage with crushing debt, you're headed for trouble from the time you exchange vows. If your partner has proven him or herself to be incapable of spending judiciously and saving well, then trust me: somewhere out there is a better match for you.

CHAPTER 5

ESTABLISH YOUR FINANCIAL INDEPENDENCE

I meet a lot of interesting people in television. Most of them are decent, well-intentioned men and women who are trying hard to provide for their families. But they haven't always made the best decisions. For some, one bad choice was enough to put them on the road to financial ruin.

Katrina is a 40-year-old woman who immigrated to Canada as a teenager. She is intelligent and industrious, and as she told me her story, I was shocked that someone so bright could be in such serious financial trouble—all because of one crucial mistake.

Katrina had gone to university, studied hard, and was working as a teacher when she met Raj, her husband, through an arranged match. Raj was a charismatic young man and an up-and-coming engineer. The two hit it off immediately. It took some time for

Raj to pass due diligence with Katrina's family. Her mother was concerned that he was in his mid-20s and had not amassed much in the way of savings, but eventually both families gave the relationship the green light. Raj and Katrina worked hard during the first years of their marriage to save money and invest wisely. Raj handled all the family finances, and little by little, their dynasty began to grow. Six years later, they were ready to start a family. Because Raj had greater earning potential, they decided he would continue to work while she would stay at home with the children. Before long, Katrina had her hands full raising three rambunctious boys. She took care of the house and found immense joy in being a mother, and Raj continued managing the family finances as he had always done. Everything was going well . . . until it wasn't.

Something Katrina had always loved about Raj was his ability to dream big and get excited about things. But Raj's enthusiasm came at a cost: he was constantly coming up with ideas for striking it rich with some hare-brained business scheme. Katrina had always been the more practical partner; in the beginning, she was able to talk him down from his get-rich-quick delusions. But as she became increasingly involved with the kids, she lost track of what her husband was doing with their money. Unbeknownst to her, Raj had made some very bad investments.

It started when he bought some risky stock. One of the guys at work was going on and on about a mining company in Chile that was about to hit it big; he told Raj he'd be a fool not to invest. Never wanting to miss out on a good thing, Raj siphoned some money out of the couple's joint account. When Katrina noticed something awry on the bank statements, he lied and told her he'd needed the money to buy some materials for work. He got angry and accused her of not trusting him, so she swallowed her misgivings and said nothing. A few years later, he suggested they move into a bigger house. Katrina was skeptical, but Raj assured her he had done the math and that they could afford the increased mortgage payments and corresponding costs. She wanted to ask *how* they could afford it—Raj hadn't been given a raise in five years—but she bit her tongue, trying, as always, to be supportive. When they missed a house payment, she asked if she could go with him the next time he saw their financial advisor. He scoffed. "Don't be ridiculous, Kat. We can't afford to pay a babysitter for the kids just so you can keep an eye on me. That's fiscally irresponsible." So Katrina was silent.

The couple started to bleed money. One day, Katrina couldn't buy groceries because the credit card had been maxed out. She tried the debit card and it, too, was declined. She drove home in a daze, her kids screaming in the back seat. When she arrived home, she went to the family computer and tried to log into the bank account she shared with Raj. Then she realized she didn't know the password. She had never needed it before because her husband handled all of their accounts. Katrina had no relationship whatsoever with their financial institution. And because Raj had never let her go with him to see their CPA or financial advisor, she didn't even know their names.

"But that wasn't the worst thing, Kevin," she told me, her face grave. "For as long as we have been married, we have filed a joint tax return. It has been over a decade since I made my own income, but I always signed my name to the return. This year, Raj was found to owe $45,000 in back taxes. Every piece of furniture we own, our car, our home—it was all purchased with Raj's income. That means they can take it all away from us. And I am liable as well."

I wanted to tell Katrina that her husband's bad money management wouldn't affect her. But unfortunately, I could not. She was right: both Raj *and* Katrina were on the hook for $45,000. The Canada Revenue Agency could go after them however they pleased. And when money owed to the CRA went into collections, I knew what would happen: they'd stop at nothing to get it. They might freeze the couple's bank accounts, seize the car or the house, or even harass Katrina with phone calls and visits while her husband was at work.

What was Katrina's crucial mistake? You might say "marrying Raj," and I wouldn't argue with you. But really, this wasn't the main mistake. Enough due diligence had been done by Katrina and her family to investigate Raj's financial past; it was his future that had become the problem. Katrina's mistake came after she was married. She allowed herself to become disenfranchised from the family dynasty and from knowledge of the family coffers. She let Raj make every single decision pertaining to money, and unfortunately for their whole family, he made some lousy ones.

You must be financially aware before your marriage and during it—you can't afford not to be. I don't care how capable you think your spouse is; you can lose everything in an instant if he or she screws up. Katrina was behind the scenes, working hard to keep the family happy and healthy, while her husband was out losing every cent of their hard-earned money. Had Katrina carved out her own business relationship with an independent financial advisor, she would have been able to protect herself *and* her kids. She might even have been able to steer Raj away from some very poor money decisions.

Money Mistake: *You Don't Have Your Own Financial Advisor*
The Fix: *Get One, Stat*

In my last book, I talked about your Secret 10. That's the 10 percent of your income that you're putting away and saving for later. I encouraged you to start saving that money while you were young and to keep growing it after you got married. Protecting your Secret 10 is the first step toward financial independence.

But now I'm taking it a step further. What do you do with your Secret 10 once it has grown into a substantial nest egg? How do you invest those funds? Simple: if you're not a financial expert yourself, you get help. You work alongside a qualified investment advisor who can put those funds to work for you. "But Kevin," you say, "we've already got an advisor. My husband (or wife) goes to see him all the time." If this were a test, you just failed it. *You must have your own investment advisor.* If you're married and you do not have an advisor independent of your partner, go out and find one this instant.

Ideally, you came into your marriage with some money. It may have been a lot or a little—whatever you'd been setting aside for your Secret 10. It is your job to ensure that money is being handled by an independent professional who is yours and yours alone. Don't entrust this job to anyone else. Think of it as your insurance policy. It shields you against financial disasters like the one Katrina experienced, and it protects you if you ever get divorced. A divorce is so much easier if you have your own advisor and your own funds; you'll be able to split your assets without missing a beat.

This isn't just a safeguard in case of divorce. Financial independence is the bedrock of a healthy partnership. Think about it:

My mother, Georgette, was an astute investor. She believed in keeping a close watch on her money. She would meet with her financial advisor often and would invest only in stocks that paid dividends and bonds with cash interest. She drilled into my head the mantra "Never spend the principal, only the interest." Today O'Leary Funds is built on this simple but effective principle.

your partner is your equal, and a good relationship is built on a healthy system of checks and balances. We've already said that money is the number one reason couples break up. Why on earth would you want to create an imbalance in such an important area? Being financially dependent on your partner is like playing with matches: you're both going to get burned. Instead, you should have your own accounts, your own relationships with financial institutions and your own stocks and bonds—even if it's just a small amount. You are essentially creating your own financial infrastructure as a kind of safety net.

I wish more women would heed this advice. I think it's a tragedy that so many married women—even those with very successful careers—shy away from the family finances. Independent agency Maddock Douglas recently surveyed over 600 women ages 21 to 59. *Ninety percent* of these women weren't sure how much money to invest or what type of investment accounts to open, and 84 percent lacked faith in their ability to set and meet specific financial benchmarks.

If you're a woman reading this book, please: break the trend! You don't have to go it alone—that's why you team up with a really good investment advisor who can steer you in the right direction. I'm here to tell you that you not only *can* do it, you must. I've said before that I believe women make better investors than men, and I stand by that. They tend to be more conservative than men—they're less risk-oriented. Women often have the ability to step back and take a more comprehensive and nuanced view. And yet, so often they are put in a position where they don't control the family's finances. That's a huge mistake.

Ladies, you are not hurting your marriage by having your own accounts and advisors or by being money-conscious; you're actually helping it. There's no need to be clandestine. Tell your partner what you're doing and why. All you're doing is forcing diversification. Trust me: that's a good thing.

Once you're ready to work with a financial advisor, you'll need to decide whether to hire a planner or a broker. These aren't synonymous—they actually do two different things. Planners can help you with life insurance and tax savings, but as far as investments go, they can buy only mutual funds, whereas a broker can buy stocks and bonds. The Mutual Fund Dealers Association of Canada (MFDA) regulates planners; brokers are regulated by the Investment Industry Regulatory Organization of Canada (IIROC). Each has specialized knowledge: planners can help you with life insurance and tax planning, whereas brokers focus more on trading stocks and creating an investment portfolio. All banks have brokerage arms; they do not have planner arms.

My suggestion? If your spouse has a broker, get a financial planner. If your spouse has a financial planner, get a broker. If your husband has an account at the local bank, open your account elsewhere. Now you've got independence *and* diversification—the best of both worlds.

———

At some point in your life, you have to pass the tipping point where you stop paying interest to others because you are in debt and you start collecting interest and dividends because you have begun to invest. Your nest egg and the income it provides are what you are going to live off when you get old and crusty!

Investors are always asking me how they can avoid paying fees to have their investments managed. You can't. The investment advisory business is a multibillion-dollar industry. None of the people in it work for free. If you elect to use a broker or financial planner, you should know with certainty that they are going to get paid a fee to perform their services. The key is to get your money's worth.

A good investment advisor forces you to diversify your investments. Diversification is so important in investing, yet so many people suffer devastating losses by not implementing this simple strategy. You probably know someone who fell in love with a stock as they watched it soar in value and come to represent a large percentage of their net worth, only to ride it all the way back down as the company blew up. Remember Nortel?

I made this very mistake in my early days as an investor, but I learned the hard way and now I possess a steely discipline that is forged from the searing flames of experience.

I have already shared with you in my first and second books some basic rules that have saved my portfolio many times over the last few decades. But here is a new and more complete summary of some of my investment philosophy.

THE O'LEARY INVESTMENT PHILOSOPHY

1. **Never let a stock, bond, commodity or *any* investment become more than 5 percent of your portfolio.** It's simple advice but very effective.
2. **Never purchase a stock or bond that does not pay a dividend or interest.** In the last 40 years, over 70 percent of stock market returns have come from dividends, not capital appreciation. Shareholders of RIM, the maker of BlackBerry smart phones, watched their stock rocket to the stratosphere, only to have it crash down when the company flew too close to the sun. RIM never returned a dime to shareholders from the day it went public because it never paid a dividend. Ironically, if RIM shareholders had abided by my rule, they would still have most of their capital gains because they would have kept selling the stock as it went over 5 percent of their portfolio. A good financial advisor would have forced that discipline on them.
3. **Keep a balanced portfolio.** For years, I have kept my investments approximately 50 percent in stocks and 50 percent in bonds. When markets get volatile, the bonds provide the stability and income I want to ride out the storm. I sleep better at night with this 50/50 model. The problem is which stocks and bonds to buy and when to sell them. This is where a good investment advisor really earns his or her fees. For example, when interest rates are going down, it's good to own 10-year government bonds, but when rates are going up, you can get killed in long-duration bonds. In periods when rates are rising, it's generally good to own only short-duration bonds that mature in the near future or floating-rate ones that pay more interest as rates go up.

COLD HARD TRUTH ON FAMILY, KIDS & MONEY

Again, a good investment advisor will know this and will modify your portfolio accordingly.

I have never been a good stock or bond picker; that's why I co-founded O'Leary Funds. Today, I use my own mutual funds to provide the diversity I need. I let the professional portfolio managers pick the stocks and bonds that I own, and I get a dividend and/or interest check every month. It makes me feel warm and fuzzy when I see that cash coming in. You don't have to buy O'Leary Funds to acquire these benefits; there are many other good mutual funds available, run by terrific managers who know how to preserve and grow capital. What matters most is performance. A good investment advisor knows how to analyze mutual fund composition and performance and will help you make sound fund selections.

So, now that you know the secret of sustainable investing, you have to decide whether you are prepared to execute these strategies yourself or use the services of an investment advisor. The cold hard truth is that most people are not good at managing their own money. They lack the skill, discipline or time to get the job done. If you fall into this group, and most people do, you need to work with an advisor.

SIX RULES FOR FINDING A GOOD FINANCIAL ADVISOR

Here are six rules that I know will help you find a good advisor.

1. **Be prepared to meet and interview a lot of candidates.** When it comes to choosing an investment advisor, don't rush. People who

inherit large sums of money sometimes feel compelled to invest it all right away. If this happens to you (and I hope it does!), slow down. Starting a relationship with an advisor is like getting married: you want to think it through. Meet with at least five advisors, preferably from different firms, before you make your decision. Ask your friends for recommendations. Don't be afraid to call advisors; trust me when I say they can't wait to hear from you! Look for someone you feel comfortable with, who has a good track record of preserving capital and is willing to work within the guidelines you provide.

2. **Do a background check.** Don't be embarrassed to check out your advisor's credentials. Remember, it's *your* money we are talking about here. Going online makes it easy, since almost all stockbrokers and financial advisors can be researched using the North American Securities Administrators Association's database at NASAA.org. There are over 900,000 individuals, located across Canada and the United States, in the database. If you can't find your stockbroker or financial advisor in this database, it's a big red flag.

3. **Choose an advisor with a proven track record.** As the chairman of O'Leary Funds, I meet thousands of financial advisors and stockbrokers every year. I've met great advisors, male and female. What's most important is choosing someone you're comfortable with and are certain will do a good job. Very often, successful investment advisors form teams. This happens when their assets under management grow into the billions. You often find women on these teams because they are excellent at preserving capital and providing returns for their clients. I'm not saying women are always better advisors; all I'm saying is that many have a proven track record of success in this industry, and if you've got a good team on your side, you're always going to be in a better position to gain.

4. **Diversify advisors, too.** If you are a couple, never put both your accounts with the same advisor or financial services firm. You need to have your own relationship with an advisor, with no conflict of interest. Even if you never separate or divorce, the diversification that two accounts in two different firms provides is better than having all your family's money in one institution managed by the same person.

5. **Understand return on capital vs. return *of* capital.** In order to get returns, advisors must take risks with your capital, but if they're taking excessive risks, you're not going to have your capital returned. Ask your advisor to show you a model portfolio and see what is in it. Does the portfolio have more than 5 percent in any one investment? Is it mostly comprised of 50 percent dividend-paying stock and 50 percent interest-bearing bonds? If so, that's a good start. Now ask for the advisor's track record to see how they have performed after fees. In most cases, you're going to be paying between 1 and 2 percent in fees on the money you ask your advisor to manage. If the advisor has been providing good performance and preserving capital simultaneously, it's worth it.

6. **Monitor performance and fees.** The institution that your investment advisor works for is going to send you a statement every month. Read it. You want to monitor two metrics. First, check to see that your capital is being preserved while you are being paid dividends and interest. Second, check that your advisor is sticking to the rules you both agreed to when you started working together. For example, has any holding in your portfolio grown over a 5 percent weighting, and are you still 50 percent in stocks and 50 percent in bonds? I recommend that you meet with your advisor at least twice a year to go over your portfolio in person, and never hesitate to pick up the phone and call if you have a question. That's service you're paying for.

If you follow these rules and you keep your spending within reason while you are retired, you will sleep with the comfort that your money will outlive you. This will guarantee that people will show up for the reading of your will!

Money Mistake: *The House, Boat or Vacation Property Is in Your Name*
The Fix: *All Assets Should be Jointly Owned*

While I strongly urge you to keep your own accounts and work with your own investment advisor, if you are married I suggest doing exactly the opposite with regard to your assets. This is where you tag-team it—especially with the big purchases. It is absolutely imperative when you and your partner buy a home that it be in both of your names. Never let your spouse tell you it's better if it's only in your name because of the liabilities of his or her job. For example, let's say your wife is in a high-risk profession. Maybe she's a plastic surgeon at perpetual risk of a medical malpractice suit. Together you find the perfect house, and she entreats you to put it in your name to keep the family's biggest asset safe.

While she may be well intentioned, it's not a smart move. You never want to get into a situation where only one of you is entitled to that asset. That goes for everything you own. All of your family assets should be purchased under joint ownership, including vacation properties, boats and anything else you're buying. That way, there's no question of who gets what in the case of divorce. In the unfortunate event that you have to sell your assets, the proceeds will be split clean down the middle with fewer expensive legal fees to prove who owns what.

Money Mistake: *Your Family Assets Aren't Protected from External Forces*
The Fix: *Form a Trust*

"But Kevin," you say, "what if my husband gets sued and we lose our home because it's in his name?" My solution is simple: form a trust. A trust is a separate legal entity, much like a corporation in that it has its own trustees, its own benefactors and beneficiaries, and its own rules. Who gets to define those rules? You do. You determine how the trust will operate while you're alive and after you're gone. Then you put it in the hands of the trustees, ensuring that the assets remain out of your creditors' reach while still keeping them within your family's control. A trust can't be pierced by divorce or litigation. I've set up a bunch of different trusts for my family: the 1997 O'Leary Family Trust names Linda and the kids as beneficiaries, and then I did a separate one for just Savannah and Trevor. It's a great way to protect our family assets in perpetuity.

Let's say you decide to create a trust for your children. You move the family home into the trust, defining the mandate and who will manage it. After that, it doesn't change for generations. Your home is safe. Another beautiful thing about putting your house into a trust is that it precludes a lot of messy family quarrels after you've passed away. Your siblings, kids and stepkids can't fight for the assets. Even if they are beneficiaries of the trust, they don't have the right to dissolve it. Putting your house in a trust forces you to define exactly who gets what before there's a divorce or a death in the family. If you and your spouse get embroiled in a nasty custody battle someday, your assets will be protected. The trustees won't get emotional about who did what to whom. Their job is simply to follow the rules you and your partner mutually agreed on from the get-go.

I don't care how much money you've got, putting your home into a trust is a great way to protect your biggest asset. It's an excellent tool for the family dynasty because if forces you to have a healthy discussion about what could and should happen down the road. A trust makes you deal with the future today.

There are other strategies for protecting your assets, so you'll want to consult your lawyer and/or financial advisor about the options available to you. Again, it's all a matter of being financially aware the minute you're married—and preferably long before.

Money Mistake: *You Think You and Your Partner Are Exempt Because You're Different*
The Fix: *Same-Sex and Common-Law Partnerships—Same Rules Apply*

Everything I'm saying goes for same-sex couples and common-law partners as well. Keep your money safe, no matter whom you shack up with. Whether you get married in a church, a courthouse or on the island of Tahiti; whether you get hitched to a man or a woman; whether your marriage license is hot off the press or you're joined together by common law; the financial implications are identical. Each person in the relationship should have his or her own bank account and his or her independent financial advisor. If you're building a life together, build it together financially. Work hard to grow your financial dynasty, and put assets in both of your names. That's the tie that binds.

Build your partnership the way you'd build a business: with sound financial decisions and investments of both money and time. Why not make your collaboration financial? After all, you're partners. The more you have invested in staying together—figuratively and financially—the harder it will be to separate. This doesn't minimize your marriage; it actually helps strengthen it. And it doesn't mean you are dependent or codependent; what you're trying to establish is *inter*dependence, where you both have equal but separate financial identities. If you structure your partnership in this way, you'll honor your commitment to one another by focusing on what really matters: finding lasting financial freedom.

I started this chapter by telling you about Katrina, who, two years later, is still trying to dig herself and her children out of debt. I'd like to end it by telling you a very different tale: the story of a woman I met on *Dragons' Den* who is the polar opposite of disenfranchised.

Esther emigrated from China 15 years ago with her husband, Ed. She's always had a head for numbers. In fact, the couple decided early on that Esther would handle the family finances, because even Ed knew she was far better with money than he was. It was Esther who started the arduous process of applying to immigrate to Canada while she and Ed were living in Shanghai, and thanks to her diligence, their move to Canada was eventually approved.

They met the challenge with gusto, working a variety of jobs— most of which they were overqualified for—to save money. Their work ethic was tremendous, and they made many personal sacrifices to amass a bit of cash, including living in a one-room apartment. Esther counted every penny going in and every penny going out. In six months, they had paid off the loan they had taken out to finance their move. Six months after that, the couple had accrued a small nest egg. Esther watched with pleasure as the money in their accounts began to grow.

That's right: *accounts*. Plural. Esther had always had her own money. She had brought it from China, and as soon as she and Ed arrived in Canada, she wasted no time setting up her own account. There was the joint account she shared with Ed, of course, which she monitored closely, but 10 percent of the money she earned went into a separate account that was hers alone. As their savings grew, Ed made an appointment with an investment advisor to start building a portfolio. Esther made an appointment, too—with a different advisor. She ultimately interviewed three advisors before settling on one she liked: a woman named Beth. Beth's investment strategy made a lot of sense to Esther, and it centered on two points: be conservative, and diversify. Under Beth's guidance, Esther's investment portfolio began to prosper.

During Ed and Esther's fifth year in Toronto, Esther became pregnant. At the same time, they were presented with a unique business opportunity: to purchase a traditional Chinese bakery. They spent many days weighing the pros and cons, discussing it with one another and with their independent advisors. To their delight, their scrupulous saving and judicious investing had paid off. They were able to sell some stocks to get the liquidity they needed to make a down payment. The couple agreed to buy the bakery under two conditions: they would make the purchase under a joint ownership, and Esther would continue to handle the finances. They would approach the business the same way they had always approached their marriage: Esther would keep the books and monitor the cash flow to ensure the business was profitable. During those early months of running the business, Esther would often bring the crib into the office and balance the books at night while her newborn slept!

The bakery, whose sales had been flagging under the prior owner, began to flourish under the watchful eyes of both husband and wife. They understood their market, and they catered to it wisely. By the company's third year, they could boast almost a million in sales. By the fifth year, that figure had more than doubled. Esther and Ed split the profits 50/50: they each got 50 cents of every dollar. In other words, they got rich, separately and together. Because they were financially stable, they were able to bring other family members to Canada to help grow the business. Esther brought her mother over from China to provide childcare for their blossoming family (by this point, she had two young children). Ed brought his brother, who was a master pastry chef back home. With his help, the bakery got write-ups in several newspapers and food blogs, bringing more attention to them and their products.

By the time I met Esther, the bakery was a smash hit. She and Ed had opened two additional locations in Toronto and were seeking capital to expand into other provinces. I looked at the cash flow and was blown away. Needless to say, I was very interested in their business plan!

I asked Esther how she did it—how she never failed to make smart financial choices that catapulted her and her husband from rags to riches in a little over a decade. "Financial independence for both partners, in perpetuity," she told me, with a sly smile. "Isn't that the way?"

Esther didn't need me to give her advice. She was money-wise all on her own. In fact, she was financially aware the minute she got married—and every minute since. Best of all, she used her money smarts to strengthen her partnership with Ed. They didn't just build a marriage. They built a family dynasty that will provide security and happiness for many years to come.

QUIZ: ARE YOU FINANCIALLY INDEPENDENT IN YOUR MARRIAGE?

Whose story sounds most like yours—Katrina's or Esther's? My goal is to help you move toward Esther on the financial independence spectrum. To figure out exactly how independent or dependent you are, try the quiz below.

1. Do you have a separate savings and/or checking account from your partner or spouse?   Y/N
2. Are you aware of the various financial products available to you, and have you invested diversely across stocks, bonds, GICs and mutual funds?   Y/N
3. Do you have an independent investment advisor managing only your portfolio, separate from your partner's?   Y/N
4. Are your family assets purchased under a joint ownership? This includes your house, vacation properties, boats, recreational vehicles and any equipment or property you own for the family business.   Y/N
5. If your spouse runs a family business, is he or she valuating your contribution? (I mean that quite literally—you should be making a percentage of every dollar your spouse makes in the business, and if you contribute equally, that percentage should be equal, too. Even if you've been a homemaker for the past 30 years, you've been making a huge contribution to the family dynasty, and you deserve to be paid for it.)   Y/N

If you answered yes to most of these questions, hats off to you. You are achieving financial independence. But don't get complacent: I encourage you to continue to seek diversification in your portfolio and work alongside your partner to keep building your financial dynasty.

If you've answered a mix of yes and no, you've got some work to do when it comes to protecting your financial future. As of right now, your financial independence is not secure. If you have your own investment advisor, schedule a review to see what could be improved. If you don't have your own advisor, hire one.

If you answered mostly no to these questions, you may be heading into a financial catastrophe. The good news: it's not too late to avert it. Set up an appointment today with a financial advisor and investigate the options that are available to you. Knowledge is a powerful tool. The only one who can rescue you from financial dependency is you.

CHAPTER 6

BUILD THE BEDROCK OF YOUR PARTNERSHIP

A strong financial foundation is the first step to building your family dynasty. So how do you construct one? We've talked about the big-picture items—financial independence, joint ownership of assets, putting the family home into a trust. But how about the day-to-day? How do you and your partner shore up the bedrock of your partnership so that you can live the kind of life you want to live? The answer is easy: you plan for it.

I once worked as a bricklayer—I'll tell you all about it in chapter 8—so I know a thing or two about building a structure that's made to last. Before you start laying bricks, you measure. You use a tape measure to determine the length and width of the wall, and then you stake out the size of it. You check and double-check your numbers, and when you're absolutely sure you've got it right, you stretch a string around the perimeter of the stakes so that you can dig out the area. All of this happens before you ever lay the first brick.

Your partnership requires the same level of diligence. In fact, you must be even *more* diligent, because you aren't just building a wall, you're building an entire life. Setting financial goals, making a plan and sticking to a budget are the mortar that will make a solid, good life possible.

Though I advocate having separate accounts and separate investment advisors, you want to grow your financial dynasty *together*. In order for that to happen, you and your partner must have a clear idea of your current financial situation. In my last book, I showed you how to determine your 90-Day Number. This is the number you get when you add up every source of income you receive over a three-month period, and then subtract every expense you've got. This calculation is too important a step to skip, so I'm going to walk you through the process here. Below, I've included the 90-Day Number worksheet from *Men, Women & Money*. This time, I want you to complete the exercise with your partner.

Money Mistake: *You Don't Know How Much Money You Have*
The Fix: *Calculate Your 90-Day Number*

First, gather your pay stubs and your partner's. If you can't track them all down, pull up your bank statements from the last three months. Write down every source of income the two of you have, including any CPP and OAS benefits. Don't forget about tax refunds, cash from side jobs, insurance rebates, reimbursements from friends and family, PayPal payments, alimony or child support and any dividends or interest earned from your investments. We're not tabulating your assets, so leave out your car and home mortgage. Right now we're only concerned with your incoming cash flow. If it's liquid, jot it down.

90-DAY INPUT

Income/Salary (Net) _____

Child Support _____

Alimony _____

Bonuses/Winnings _____

Tax Returns/Credits _____

Interest Earned _____

Dividends Earned _____

Employment Insurance _____

Annuities _____

Inheritances _____

Other _____

Other _____

Other _____

Your 90-Day Input Number _____

Now write down all the stuff you and your partner spend money on. I'm not just talking about your rent, mortgage payment, utilities, insurance and other big-ticket items. I mean every coffee and bag of chips you've bought over the last 90 days. Haircuts, magazines, donations, gasoline, groceries, dinners out, travel expenses, smart phone apps, valet parking, that sleek new pair of shoes—every single thing. If you keep your checkbook balanced, perfect: use it to track your expenditures. Don't leave anything out. The more honest the two of you are, the more you stand to gain from this exercise.

90-DAY OUTPUT

Rent/Mortgage Payments _____

Condo Fees/Property Taxes _____

Home Repair/Upkeep _____

Child Care _____

Dependent Care _____

Education _____

Alimony _____

Veterinarian _____

Health Care (medical) _____

Health Care (dental) _____

Prescriptions _____

Health Insurance _____

Gym _____

Cosmetics _____

Personal Care (salon/spa/yoga) _____

Pet Food/Expenses _____

Car/Lease Payments _____

Insurance (car/life/home) _____

Investments _____

Taxes _____

Debt Payments _____

Gifts _____

Car Repairs _____

Gas _____

Parking _____

Public Transit _____

Cabs _____

Utilities _____

Phone _____

Home Repairs/Services _____

Cable/Internet _____

Books/Magazines/Newspapers _____

Hobbies _____

Clothing _____

Dry Cleaning _____

Groceries _____

Restaurants _____

Takeout _____

Travel _____

Entertainment/Movies/Concerts _____

Video Games _____

Computers/Repairs _____

Misc. Technology _____

Banking Fees _____

Legal/Accounting Fees _____

Home Office Supplies _____

Other _____

Other _____

Other _____

Other _____

Other _____

Other _____

Other _____

Other _____

Other _____

Your 90-Day Output Number _____

Here's where the rubber meets the road. Take your 90-Day Output Number and subtract it from your 90-Day Input Number.

Your 90-Day Input − Your 90-Day Output = Your 90-Day Number

_____ − _____ = _____

You're left with a cold hard number that's going to tell you a lot about the state of your finances. This is a way for you to take your financial temperature and determine your next steps. If your 90-Day Number is positive, you're making money and building wealth. Well done! If your 90-Day Number is in the red, you're in deep trouble. Listen carefully to Uncle Kevin, because things are about to get very bad if you don't. It's time to declare an official state of emergency. Downsize where you live. Move closer to where you work. Eliminate the car you can't afford. Stop taking vacations. You are on a path to financial ruin, and horrible things are going to happen to you if you don't make a change. You need this book very badly. Do not go out to dinner, and do not stop reading. The only thing you are allowed to spend money on is another copy of this book for your spouse!

Here's the good news: if you work hard to make up the deficit, you can regain your footing. It's not too late. Correct your bad spending habits now and you can still build a strong family dynasty. But you have to adjust *immediately* so that, by the time you calculate your number in another 90 days, you're back in the black.

I meet a lot of young couples on *Shark Tank* and *Dragons' Den*, many of whom are just starting out. Almost every single one of them is in debt. Many have bought a house together, and now they're saddled with a mortgage while still paying off their student loans. These kids have barely begun their life together and already they are struggling under the weight of thousands of dollars of debt.

I'll give you the same advice I give these couples. Right now, you have only two financial goals: get out of debt and pay off your mortgage; and keep putting 10 percent of your income into your Secret 10.

Money Mistake: *You're Bleeding Money Left and Right*
The Fix: *Honor the 90/10 Rule*

I call this the 90/10 Rule. For every dollar you earn, 90 cents should go to paying off debt, and 10 cents should go to your Secret 10. The 90/10 Rule supersedes everything until you've paid off all your debt. You don't travel. You don't buy a fancy sports car. You don't give to charity. You shouldn't even have an investment portfolio, unless that's where you put your Secret 10. My dissenters say my strategy is too myopic. "You can't really expect people to put 90 cents of every dollar toward their mortgage, Kevin," they say. "Everybody needs to let off steam." Sure they do. So you better find ways to let off steam that don't involve spending money.

Let me tell you why you should pay off your mortgage before doing anything else. The interest rate on a mortgage today is about 3.8 percent. That means *you are guaranteed to make 3.8 percent* simply by paying off a debt that costs you 3.8 percent. There is no other investment in the world that guarantees you a 3.8 percent return. Stocks and bonds are not guaranteed, as we discovered in 2008 when everything collapsed. They came back, but that's a lot of volatility. If you put all your money toward paying off your mortgage, there's no volatility and no risk. You are guaranteed a high rate of return.

Plenty of people disagree with me. In David Chilton's first book, he argued for diversification; he advised his readers to put two-thirds of their money into stocks and bonds and devote the final third to paying off their mortgage. Controversial as it may be, I don't agree with Chilton. Interest rates are only going to go up. As rates continue to increase, the argument for putting every penny toward your mortgage gets stronger. If a fixed mortgage goes up to 7 or 8 percent, your rate of return is 7 or 8 percent. Good luck getting those kinds of returns with no risk and no volatility in the stock market!

When you get a mortgage, you want to design it so that you can pay it off as soon as possible. Don't invest in anything until you've paid it off. Think of every mortgage payment as an investment in your debt-free future.

The remaining 10 cents should go toward your Secret 10. It's a tax like any other, but it's the only tax in your life that you benefit from personally. The Secret 10 is a tax just for you. It's also your Catastrophe Cash Fund. If disaster strikes and you need cash, you'll have it. That's what it's there for.

How long will it take you to pay off your mortgage? Good question. Take a look at the following chart. Let's assume you owe $200,000 and you've got a fixed-rate mortgage at 5.34 percent. You took my advice from my second book and are making biweekly payments. Here's what you'll be paying over four different amortization periods—including the total interest you'll accrue.

PAYING OFF YOUR MORTGAGE

LENGTH OF MORTGAGES	BIWEEKLY PAYMENT	TOTAL INTEREST PAID
20 years	$621.48	$48,560.24
15 years	$740.75	$46,8351.54
10 years	$987.11	$41,789.11
5 years	$1,751.21	$27,635.14

Source: Table designed using data from Mortgage Payment Calculator, TD Canada Trust, 2013.

If you can pay off your mortgage in five years instead of 10, you'll save $14,000 in interest. If you can pay off your mortgage in five years instead of 20, you'll save $21,000. But more importantly, the sooner you pay it off, the sooner you can dispense with the 90/10 Rule and save your money for other goals and even spend a little, too.

Money Mistake: *You Can't Afford a Vacation*
The Fix: *Invest Time without the Money*

You've got no business taking luxurious vacations until you've dug yourselves out of debt. In the early days of your marriage, extravagant trips will only sink you into *more* debt, which can seriously undermine your partnership. You don't want that.

But that doesn't mean you shouldn't go on vacations. There are plenty of ways to create special memories with one another without plunging into debt (flip to the end of this chapter for some ideas). One of the most fruitful ways of investing time in one another is to take a few days away and do something special, just the two of you.

I like to say there are two types of vacations. First is the Phase One Vacation. This is the romantic tryst, the adventures you have together *before* you have children. You are building a history, replete with fond recollections and nice photographs. The hope is that the more of these memories you've accrued, the harder it will be to walk away from all the rich history you've built together.

As your children get older, it gets harder to keep the family together, particularly on vacations. New relationships outside of the family are an important part of growing up. One way to keep everybody together is to invite the friends along! Here we are on a vacation in the Caribbean with my daughter, Savannah, and her friend. It might cost more, but it's worth it.

The minute your first child is born, it all changes. From now on, you bring your kids with you wherever you go. That means you're going to Disneyland and Canada's Wonderland and all the other money pits designed to put a sparkle in your child's eye (and take the money from your wallet). But you'll do it, because by the time you're planning a Phase Two Vacation, you're building the foundation of family, not just your relationship with your spouse. Children remember vacations and summer sojourns in a special way. Time spent together is a smart investment; it makes your relationship with your kids stronger, fortifying your family as a result.

Money Mistake: *You Want to Have a Bunch of Kids*
The Fix: *Have Only as Many as You Can Afford*

I'll say this until I'm blue in the face: *there is no need to enter into a marriage contract if you don't want kids.* If this describes you, you'll probably want to skip over the next few chapters of this book because the information won't apply. But if you're like most people I know, your family dynasty is going to include one or more children. The question then becomes: How many should you have?

You may not like the answer, but here it is: *have only as many children as your income can support.* Nobody wants to be told how many kids they should or shouldn't have. And yet those same people often come to me, wanting my advice on how to raise healthy, brilliant children into a world of opportunity that simply doesn't exist unless you, the parents, create it. "But Kevin," they say, "there is no greater joy than children." I agree. Which is why you deserve to give the ones you've got the absolute best shot at life. In today's world, having a whole bunch of kids may not be realistic; moreover, it may not be fair because it overtaxes your family's resources. You must balance the joys of having multiple children with the fact that those children could be living close to the poverty line as a result of your decisions.

People tend to think of children outside of the metrics of money. Most prospective parents don't take a realistic look at their budget and decide, "Yes, let's have a third child" or "You know what? Let's not." For parents who actually choose to have children, who plan to have them, this decision usually comes from an emotional place. But what I am suggesting is having at least a few thoughts where you *separate the decision to have children from the emotional need to have children.* At least try to think logically about your finances instead of just heading blindly toward dividing the family's

The faster my businesses grew, the more time I spent away from home. I decided one day that no matter what happened with work, I would always spend my weekends with my kids and wife. Here I am enjoying some "bubbly" with Trevor and Savannah when they were young.

resources between more and more mouths. The more children you have, the less they have—the less money, possibly less experiences and advantages, maybe even fewer educational opportunities. And, let's not forget: more children means less of your time, because you're busy with all the other kids and the multiple jobs you're juggling to try to keep food on the table. For every new child who shows up, you are taking a percentage of time and money away from the ones who already exist. This is why large families are a luxury of those with means. In families that suffer from severe financial burdens, having more kids does not lighten those burdens. On the contrary, *your children may inherit the burden*. That's right: instead of leaving your children an inheritance, you may actually leave them the burden of your debt.

Families that are under deep economic stress encounter big problems when kids factor into the mix. Years into your marriage, you may find that cracks in the foundation of your partnership begin to show in new and ugly ways. If your relationship was founded on poor financial planning and mismanaged money— and if your decision to have a whole brood came from a purely emotional place, rather than being carefully thought out and prepared for—your kids may be the ones who pay the cost.

So how many kids can you afford to have? It's a simple math equation. According to Statistics Canada, it costs $243,660 to raise a child to age 18. That's $1,070 a month per child. That includes almost everything—food, clothes, medical and dental costs, school, extracurriculars, transportation costs, even braces.

Now that you've got the numbers staring you in the face, there's really no excuse for poor decisions. For your future children's sake, if not your own, take a calm, rational look at your finances and ask yourself: Can we afford it? Here's where the worksheets I had you complete earlier come back into play. The number of kids you have *must be tied to your annual surplus.* Remember, that's your 90-Day Number times four. To make it easy, I've provided a chart below.

THE COST OF KIDS

	ANNUAL SURPLUS NEEDED PER YEAR
1 Child	$12,825
2 Children	$25,650
3 Children	$38,475
4 Children	$51,300
5 Children	$64,125

Keep in mind that these numbers do *not* include university tuition. If you want to send your child to university, you're looking at anywhere from $20,000 to $64,000 for a four-year degree. Thanks to inflation, that figure will go up significantly over the next 18 years, so if your wee one's still in swaddling clothes, expect to dole out anywhere between $64,000 and $137,000 for their university pedigree. If you make an annual contribution of $2,000, your child's RESP will grow to $71,166 in 18 years (based on a return of 5 percent per year and reinvestment of dividends).

You may think your children are going to take care of you in your old age, and this is a justification many people offer for having children. But many kids are too busy living their own lives (hence the surge of retirement homes and long-term care facilities) and don't have the time or means to take care of their elders. You cannot count on your kids as a security blanket for your own future. The sooner you can get that idea through your head, the better off you'll be.

Frankly, unless you're rolling in cash, I endorse having only two kids. I'm biased, of course, since I've got two great kids myself. Having more than two children becomes a financial risk with a good chance of failure. Your children will carry on your financial legacy, for better or for worse, so why not give them the best chance possible at success?

I took this picture of my daughter, Savannah, and Linda one sunny morning in Boston. I remember looking through the viewfinder and thinking about how much my life was about to change and what new responsibilities were to come. Planning on having a family? You need to think through the financial implications in tandem with the emotional ones.

Money Mistake: *You've Bought into Traditional Wisdom About Who Works and Who Stays Home*
The Fix: *Follow the Dollar Signs*

I want to comment briefly on the traditional roles of "breadwinner" and "stay-at-home parent," since we're talking about tying the number of kids you have to your income. For years, it was the father who often went out and earned a living while the mother stayed home to raise the kids. Women were relegated to the domestic realm while men worked their way up the corporate ladder, earning promotions and bigger paychecks. To this day, studies show that a woman in the workplace earns an average of 77 cents to a man's dollar.

But that's not the whole story. Many women today have successful, lucrative careers. A recent Pew report found that four in 10 households with children have a woman as the primary breadwinner, and sometimes she is the *sole* breadwinner. Fifty years ago, that statistic was one in 10. Single mothers account for many of those households today, but in over five million cases, the couple is married; the wife simply makes more than her husband.

I point this out for a reason: so that you don't get stymied by conventional expectations. Whoever can make money and wants to work should do it! At the beginning of your marriage, you're in the maximum debt—you may both be paying off your student loans, and now you have a mortgage *and* a baby. You want to make your 90-Day Number as high as you can possibly get it. If you decide to have kids, take a cold hard look at the numbers. Who has the higher earning potential? That's who goes to work. The other one works to care for the children and the house. If that means Mom goes to the office while Dad stays with baby, so be it.

Husbands: don't be threatened by your wife's earning potential. Embrace it. The money she brings home every month will shore up your financial foundation and strengthen your partnership. Wives: if you want to work, go for it! And if you want to be a working mother, do it! At no previous point in history have so many women enjoyed motherhood *and* successful careers. Strike a balance that's right for you.

FOUR AFFORDABLE PHASE ONE VACATIONS

Phase One Vacations—the trips you go on *before* you have kids—are part of the brick and mortar of a healthy partnership. The memories you make will sustain you over the coming decades. But during the early years, your goal should be to save money, not spend it. Here are four affordable vacation ideas that put a premium on the *time* you spend together, not the money.

1. **Visit a national park**. There's something majestic about being with the person you love in the wilderness. It's a chance to break out of the daily grind, unplug your smart phone and soak up the wonders of nature. Plus, it's cheap. Tent and RV camping can save you thousands on room and board. If you plan your vacation carefully, you can even swing free admission. Every year on Canada Day, entry to national parks, national historic sites and national marine conservation areas is 100 percent free. Bonus: without running water and modern creature comforts, you and your partner can't help but develop a deeper (and potentially smellier) bond.

2. **Hit the road, but not too far**. Everybody loves a good road trip. To save on gas, consider choosing a nearby destination, and be sure to check GasBuddy.com to find the cheapest price. To save on lodging, see if anyone you know will be going on their own vacation and might volunteer to let you stay in their house while they're gone. "Subletting" has all the appeal of a

hotel—you're someplace new and exotic—with more of the little luxuries you're used to (a working coffee maker, couches you can actually sit on). Early on in our relationship, Linda and I flew to California, rented a car and drove through Napa Valley on a wine tour. One of my venture capitalist friends had a gorgeous place in Sonoma and let us have it for the week. Linda and I still talk fondly about that trip. Bonus: more time in the car means more time to talk about the future.

3. **Revamp a business trip**. If your company sends you somewhere interesting, that's half the fare paid for. You can't expect work to pick up the tab for your partner's meals, but consider tacking on some vacation time before or after your trip and having your spouse meet you once your business duties are over. To this day, Linda often accompanies me on business trips; she'll come with me to Los Angeles when I'm filming *Shark Tank*. During the day, she gets to do her own thing, and at night we enjoy all that the city has to offer. Bonus: when you're on a business trip, many of the "extras" are tax-deductible for you (not for your spouse), so be sure to keep all your receipts and talk to your accountant about itemizing deductions.

4. **Have a staycation**. A "staycation" is just a vacation where you stay at home. Simply use your place as a home base for local adventures—go pick blackberries, check out a museum exhibit you've been wanting to see, or attend a nearby music festival. Back home at night, kick back, have a glass of wine and unwind. To get the most out of your staycation, turn off the ringer on your phone and set a vacation alert on your email accounts. Don't

read or watch the news. You're on vacation—no one even has to know you're still in town. Bonus: enjoy being with your partner in the comfort of your own home, *without* the normal daily stresses. You've got everything you need!

Remembering my mother's advice when it came time for Linda and me to raise our own children, we tried to keep it simple. Here are Savannah (second from right) and Trevor (second from left) enjoying ice cream cones with friends at a small general store. The most valuable commodity when raising children is time to spend with them.

PART THREE

KIDS

CHAPTER 7

GIVE YOUR KIDS AN MBA:
MONEY & BANKING AWARENESS

My daughter, Savannah, was five years old when she asked me The Question. Linda and I had just taken her out to a neighborhood pizzeria to celebrate her last day of kindergarten. The server dropped off the check, and I immediately fished out my wallet to pay for the meal. I always made a point to carry cash when my kids were growing up—I wanted them to see it come out of my wallet rather than the magical plastic credit card.

Savannah watched as I thumbed through a couple of twenties and handed them to the server. "Daddy," she said. "I always see you taking money out. But where does it come from?"

The Question. I knew she'd ask it one day, and that day had finally arrived.

"Where do you think money comes from, Savannah?" I asked.

She asked to see my wallet, so I handed it to her.

"It doesn't come from your wallet," she said.

"Smart girl," I said.

"Sometimes I see Mommy put her card into the bank machine," Savannah said. "When she pushes the buttons, money comes out."

"Savannah," I said, "I know it looks like money comes from a machine, but that's just where we store the money that we earn. If Mom and I don't earn money, the bank machine won't give us any."

It's a common problem. Our kids see us effortlessly extracting money from the bank machine. They watch us whip out our credit cards to purchase meals and entertainment. Why wouldn't they think money grows on bank machines?

That day at the pizzeria, I tried to instill in my daughter two basic principles: money doesn't just materialize—you have to work for it; and if you don't have any, sometimes you have to borrow it, and that's a bad thing. Rarely in life is debt good, so it was important to Linda and me that from an early age both our kids have a negative association with debt. Debt is as bad as drugs or alcohol—its longevity is like a disease. Savannah was only five years old, but when we talked to her about debt, she was old enough to understand the concept that bad things—like touching a hot stove or taking candy from strangers—should be avoided at all costs.

It's up to you to teach your kids about money. The teachers at school aren't going to do it, and the banks sure as hell won't—the less financially literate your child is, the more they stand to profit. The buck stops with you, and I mean that literally. Every financial interaction with your child is an opportunity to teach by example, whether you're buying groceries, paying bills or visiting your investment advisor. Pay with cash at the grocery store so that your children understand something left your wallet forever. Invite your son or daughter to sit at the table with a calculator while you settle the household accounts. Bring Johnny to your next portfolio review and let him see how your money is growing. Show your kids how you handle the family finances, and then open a healthy dialogue about why you made the decisions you did.

If you flew by the seat of your pants before you were a parent, getting by from paycheck to paycheck, *it is imperative that you change the pattern*. Financially illiterate children will probably grow into financially illiterate adults. There's no need to make lessons too complex for kids. *Don't spend too much. Mostly save. Always invest.* These are the building blocks of financial literacy. If you can teach your kids those three basic principles, they'll leave the house at 18 with their very own MBA.

Money Mistake: *Your Kids Don't Know Much About Money*
The Fix: *Give Them an MBA: Money & Banking Awareness*

Any good teacher will tell you that young children learn best if you can make the lessons practical—hence why preschool math classes do so much counting on fingers. If you want to give your children an MBA—the Money and Banking Awareness they'll come to rely on as financially literate adults—you must flesh out every financial concept with a tangible lesson. You want your kids to see *why* saving and investing money is worthwhile, and to feel profit and loss for themselves.

To help parents teach their kids about money, I've created a Cash Curriculum for children ages five to 14. I suggest tying each financial lesson to a birthday, for several reasons. A child's birthday is a momentous occasion, and money is the lifeblood of momentous occasions. Birthdays have special value for a family, and you want to imbue these financial lessons with the same kind of intrinsic value. If you can make the money lesson a part of the celebration, your son or daughter will begin to understand that financial literacy can be fun. I've addressed the following age-based advice to a daughter but it works equally well for a son.

CASH CURRICULUM FOR AGES 5–14
Age 5
Bank Day

A week before your child's fifth birthday, tell her you need help with one of her presents. It's up to you whether you confess what you're up to or keep it a surprise, but here's the gist: she's going to create a Money Bin.

The Money Bin can be a jar, bag, pot or pouch—whatever gets your child excited. If your son is into pottery, perfect: have him make a small clay pot. If your daughter is an aspiring carpenter, help her craft a small wooden box. By enrolling them in the process of creating a special place for their savings, you're underlining the importance of keeping that money safe. By the way, I tend to discourage the more traditional piggy bank. Pigs carry the connotations of sloppiness and laziness, and money awareness takes care. Financially literate adults are prudent and, above all, *active* with their money. I encourage parents to have children design their own Money Bin because you want to get your kids actively engaged with their money from the start.

On the morning of her fifth birthday, have your child bring out the Money Bin. I don't care if she's applied sparkly stickers to a

Ziploc bag: ooh and ahh over her creation. Give her a Sharpie and have her write "Meanie Money" on the Bin.

Now you are going to gift her with $100. This is a lot of money for a five-year-old—if it isn't, you're doing something wrong—but it's not all for her to spend. Sit her down and explain that you will be giving her $100 every birthday for the next five years, $90 of which can go into her Meanie Money Bin. Explain to her that meanies aren't bad; they are people who, like Mommy and Daddy, save most of their money and spend very little of it. They're meanies because they *live within their means.* The $90 of Meanie Money is hers to spend over the next year, if she must—but if she saves it instead, she will earn a much bigger reward a few years down the line. Set the parameters of that reward if you wish: a trip to a theme park, maybe, or a family vacation. The goal is to teach your children that sometimes they will need to make sacrifices until they have saved enough money to afford something they really want.

What does she do with the remaining $10? This, you can explain, is her Secret 10. For the next five years, she'll be putting 10 percent of her birthday money into her Secret 10 account. This is the savings account you've set up in trust at your bank, as you are her sponsor (and you may need to pad her $10 a bit, as most banks have a minimum requirement to open a savings account). The account will flip over into your daughter's name the day she turns 18.

To launch her Secret 10 in style, declare your daughter's fifth birthday an official Family Bank Day. Let the whole gang know this is something to get excited about. This will most likely be her bank account for the rest of her life. The $10 she deposits today will accumulate and multiply, and over the coming years, she will come to understand the value of adding to it and growing this small nest egg into one that will see her through college, marriage and building a family dynasty of her own. It's a big day, so treat it as such. Happy Bank Day!

Maybe the whole family takes a trip to the bank, or it could be something special for just you and your child. The point is to make it a rite of passage—an acknowledgement that your child has taken a big step toward adulthood. Banks can be very impressive places (make no mistake: it's your money paying for those fancy windows and vaulted ceilings). They are meant to instill equal parts fear and awe. That's good—you can work with that. Explain to your child that her money is going to be under attack from the day she's born, and the bank is leading the battle cry. It is her duty and responsibility to be aware of *every penny going in or out of that account.* Give her a ledger to help her keep track, thus getting her in the habit of diligently balancing her account. You can also point out that she will accrue a little bit of interest month by month. It won't be much, but even a few cents is exciting for a five-year-old because it's money she didn't have before.

Age 6
The Bank Machine
On your child's sixth birthday, gift her with another $100. Reiterate the rules from the previous year—10 percent goes to the Secret 10, the rest is Meanie Money. Then offer to take the whole family out to dinner.

On the way to the restaurant, ask your child The Question: "Where does money come from?" Take the opportunity to open a family-wide dialogue, moderated by you and your partner. If you

© Concept/author David Johnston, "The Amazing Mister J–Magician" (www.misterj.ca). Illustrator: André Myette.

You know you're doing something right when you start showing up in comic books as a superhero! That's me using the power of money to save the world!

have other kids, invite them to join in. Stress the fact that money is something you work for; every dollar represents a commensurate amount of toil and sweat. I once knew a man who had his kids haul buckets of stones across the backyard for a home improvement project. He set an amount for each bucket: 10 cents per haul. After several days of this, his kids began to think in terms of "That piece of candy would cost 20 buckets" or "That new video game would take 300 buckets." Suddenly, money became very labor-defined!

For tonight, you're going to illustrate this point with bucks instead of buckets. Before you arrive at the restaurant, stop at a bank machine (you'll be paying for dinner in cash). Have your child watch you enter your PIN and take out a certain amount of money. Put her in charge of counting the money to make sure it's all there. Then explain to her, in as much detail as possible, how hard you had to work for that money—in other words, the intangible costs you accrued to earn it. "Remember when I went on a business trip last weekend and didn't see you for three days? On that trip I earned X amount." Or, "I worked 10 hours straight at the shop last week and was so tired I could hardly see straight. That day I made X much." The goal is to draw a direct line between the money she's holding in her hand and what you sacrificed to earn it. These are invaluable discussions, and you'll never get a chance to have them again. Even at six, kids are old enough to understand the concepts of work and sacrifice.

Enjoy dinner with your family. When it's time to pay the bill, make sure your daughter sees you pay with the crisp new bills. If you've done your job, your child no longer sees money as UFOs—Undefined Frivolous Objects. Those twenties you just gave up were a direct result of your hard work . . . and they ain't comin' back.

Age 7
The Grocery Store

This year, instead of going out to a restaurant, you're going to make birthday dinner at home. Engage your seven-year-old in planning the meal. Maybe she wants to have "breakfast for dinner," with blueberry muffins and bacon, or she wants to help Dad with a new recipe. Whatever it is, sit down with her to make a grocery list of the ingredients you'll need. Set a specified budget for the meal (and define "budget" when she gives you a blank look). Whether it's $25, $50 or $100, put the money on the table and have her count it out so she knows exactly what she's working with. Make it clear she's the one in charge. "You can spend $60 at the store. You can buy whatever you need, just as long as you don't go over budget."

Then, take the whole family to the grocery store. Put your daughter in charge of the shopping. By age seven, most kids can do simple addition and subtraction, though you may need to help a little. If you like, give her a calculator. The other family members—siblings, spouse, you—are there as her support team. Put someone in charge of recording the price of everything your daughter puts into the cart; have them keep a running tally on a big yellow legal pad. Have someone else provide color commentary, suggesting strategies when your daughter gets stuck. "The name-brand flour costs $6.99, or you could get the same size of the store brand for only $4.99." Be sure to give her a warning when she's within $10 of her target, and another warning when she's within $5. And don't forget to leave her a cushion for tax and to explain what that is! Set a family goal: to have a great meal and not go over budget no matter what.

Maybe your daughter sees a bakery cake that she really, *really* wants, or a piece of her favorite candy in the checkout line. It's your job to keep her on task. Explain that getting that cake or that piece of candy means *not* getting the ingredients you need for dinner; you'd actually have to take something out of the cart and put it back on the shelf. Teach the lesson that getting what she wants means depriving the family of something it needs. It may sound harsh, but she needs to understand that good money management means making sacrifices.

Make dinner as a family and enjoy the fruits of your labor. And don't forget to make the annual contribution of $100 to her Meanie Money Bin. After today, she'll appreciate that gift all the more.

Age 8
Bring-Your-Child-to-Work Day

This year, you're going to plan something special in addition to the $100 gift. The night before your child's eighth birthday, help her lay out her clothes for the next day. Mutually agree on a morning ritual—a quick breakfast, maybe, or fresh-pressed waffles if you've got the time. The next morning, pour her a glass of chocolate milk while you have your coffee. You'll both benefit from a little extra kick, because today is bring-your-son-or-daughter-to-work day.

This is an important day in your child's life. Sure, there's the official "take-your-kid-to-work day," but I took, my son, Trevor, to work with me at O'Leary Funds and O'Leary Mortgages much more than once a year. Guess what? He loved it. He toured the office, talked to employees and saw how the businesses worked, and it raised a lot of questions for him.

O'Leary Funds is an exciting place, especially to an eight-year-old. There are two rows of machines flickering global data non-stop. We have TVs set to all the big stations around the world: BBC, CNBC, CBC. Trevor's eyes widened as he took it all in.

"What are all those screens?" he asked.

"We're watching every market in the world," I explained. "We're buying and selling stocks in countries around the world."

Trevor looked impressed.

"See that man over there?" I said. "He's one of our dedicated employees. He's been here since 4 A.M."

"Does he work all night?"

"Sometimes. Have you ever heard of Tokyo Risk?"

Trevor shook his head.

"Investors don't like to go to bed in New York with any strings left untied, because if something happens in Tokyo while they're sleeping, everything could change. So that's why this guy works strange hours—to keep a close eye on our funds."

I walked Trevor down the hall to O'Leary Mortgages. Rick, one of our top employees, had just gotten off the phone with a woman who wanted an insured mortgage. Rick gave us her story in a nutshell: "She wants a $350,000 mortgage to buy a condominium."

Trevor's jaw dropped. "But that's so much money!"

"Yes, it is," Rick said, and then explained the woman's situation. She was 26 years old and had been at her job for a year and a half after a series of temporary positions. She was looking at a mortgage that would have her paying at least $1,800 a month, and she was only bringing in $2,600 of income. Even my eight-year-old son could see the problem.

"Don't give her the money, Dad!"

I assured Trevor that we work closely with our clients to ensure they don't bite off more than they can chew. That day made a big impression on Trevor; he still talks about it. On one hand, he saw money growing; on the other, he saw the potential dangers of losing it all. He also saw that I worked for a living.

By taking your child to work, you have the opportunity to have an enduring impact on his or her perceptions of what it's like to have a job. It should be stimulating and fun, though not *too* fun—it's supposed to be a job, not a day at the theme park. By the time it's over, your child should have a better understanding that this is what you do every day to earn money, and if you didn't, there wouldn't be food in the fridge or birthday cake on the table.

Age 9
Money Games

Assuming your child lives on planet earth, she's going to be hip to computers by age nine, possibly hipper than you! Use this to your advantage. There are all sorts of games and software designed to teach kids financial literacy. I should know—I made a fortune selling children's educational software in the 1990s. Millions of kids around the world learned simple math with Math Rabbit, one of SoftKey's best-selling products. Today there are dozens of computer games where kids have to work toward certain goals; often their avatars must complete specific tasks to earn money and rewards. This kind of role play can be extremely helpful in teaching your child how to set goals and meet them. And, of course, if you're technology-averse, there's always Monopoly. It's a great game; it encourages an understanding of money, property ownership and banking. Oh, and going bankrupt or to jail—two outcomes even the youngest children playing come to understand as negatives.

All of this role-playing around finances should help your child learn to *strategize*.

At the 1988 Comdex Conference in Las Vegas. This is one of the earliest pictures I have from my SoftKey Software Products start-up days. The dot matrix printers seen here are most likely on display at the Smithsonian! SoftKey went on to become The Learning Company, which was eventually sold to Mattel for $4.2 billion.

This is going to come in handy, because the day she turns nine you're going to sit down for a little chat. If she has saved every penny you've given her over the last five years, she should have a full $450 in her Meanie Money Bin. If she's done this, she deserves a pat on the back. That's a lot of money! If she hasn't—if she's spent some of her Meanie Money along the way—that's okay, too. But here's where she benefits from her own good money management: that $450 is going straight toward the special prize or reward you agreed on four years ago. Time to hit up that theme park or go to the fancy hotel she loves. And she's going to fund the family adventure!

If she's depleted her Meanie Money over the last four years, she may ask if there's a way to earn some of it back. It's up to you to decide how. As I said in my last book, I don't believe in a traditional allowance because your kids should be doing their designated household chores for free. Instead, brainstorm some tasks that are separate and distinct from their regular contributions to the household, perhaps washing the car, taking out a pet on walks or doing some simple gardening or spring cleaning. Devise ways for her to earn that money dollar by dollar (or, if you're a real taskmaster, quarter by quarter). Also, your suggestions for tasks are great, but take the opportunity to open a dialogue with your child about skills she has to offer. This is a great way to get your kid to start thinking about her own abilities and monetizing them. After all, these are baby steps designed to stimulate thinking about future jobs and careers.

Oh, and one more thing: you can ditch the Money Bin. She's outgrown it.

Age 10
The Bank Card

At 10, your child is moving into a new stage; you don't have to hold her hand. She knows where money comes from, and hopefully by now she has a genuine appreciation for the fact that money is something you earn, not that you are given. The lessons you impart over the next four years can be a little more complex.

Unless she launched her own start-up in fifth grade, your daughter's bank account probably hasn't seen a lot of action. That's okay. The goal is to train her how to monitor her money. If she has shown herself to be financially responsible, she may be ready for a prepaid bank card. I suggest a *prepaid* card because it allows you to maintain control—you can add money in increments as small as $5. You can also link the card directly to her savings account, so that any money she spends is her own. Most banks these days have an online dashboard; if possible, set your child up with her own password and encourage her to monitor her account balance. This gives her an easy, fun way to keep track of her money.

Remind her to monitor her account closely. The minute she starts using a bank card, the chances of being a victim to fraud multiply exponentially. You can find plenty of stories online, and members of your family probably have their own anecdotes— times your credit card was hacked or someone withdrew $500 using your debit card number even though your debit card never left your possession. Explain to your daughter that many of today's thieves use something called skimming: they affix a small device to a bank machine or pay-at-the-pump terminal that reads the data from your card's magnetic strip when you swipe it. Later, these stolen card numbers are physically attached to substitute cards, which are then used to make purchases or withdraw money from your account. Scary stuff.

Make sure your daughter understands that you're not trying to scare her. You're simply trying to prepare her for the real world. She's not a baby anymore, and now that she has a bank card, she has to be ready to take preemptive action. Here are three tips for keeping her financial information safe:

1. Make sure the bank has your family's updated contact information. Most banks have gotten pretty good at flagging suspicious charges, but they can't ask you about one if they don't have your correct phone number and email address.

2. Stay away from bank machines that appear dirty or broken— these may be fake machines set up to capture card information. If a machine asks you to enter your PIN twice, cancel the transaction immediately.

3. Always cover the keypad when you key in your PIN. It'll keep you safe from wandering eyes and any cameras that may be watching.

Again, the best way for your daughter to protect herself against theft or fraud is to be constantly vigilant and financially aware.

Age 11
E.T.s: Entrepreneurs in Training

By 11, most kids get the itch to make money. Tommy down the street has a paper route; Tina babysits on the weekends. Your child, too, has probably expressed a desire to earn a little dough. Encourage her to find safe ways to provide goods or services to the community. That could mean walking dogs, mowing lawns or pet-sitting for friends or family who are out of town. She could offer to clean an elderly neighbor's garage or pull weeds in a neglected garden. I've known kids who make their own jewelry or decorate candles, then turn around and sell their creations for a profit. I call them little E.T.s—Entrepreneurs in Training.

A friend of mine has a daughter who was an E.T.: she launched her first business at age 11. Her house was situated on a perfect corner lot, exactly one block from the local high school. The junior high let out at 3:30, while the high school let out at 3:45. She decided to make good use of those 15 minutes. Every day, she rushed home and set up a table in front of her house where she'd display popular brands of candy, chips and cookies. She'd also dump two 12-packs of soda into an ice-cold cooler. As soon as the high school final bell sounded, a steady stream of hungry and thirsty students walked right by her table—and couldn't resist. She made a tidy profit selling snacks and soda at a 300 percent markup! That is brilliant. That is entrepreneurship at its best. Today, this young woman is a recent college graduate, on the lookout for jobs in a tough market. The good news: she's been training herself to have a competitive edge from an early age! When I talked to her about her E.T. days, this is what she said: "Selling pop and candy at my corner stand was the best and easiest money I ever made!"

If your child has an entrepreneurial streak, nurture it. Help her find ways to market her business with flyers, e-blasts or word of mouth. There's nothing more exciting to an 11-year-old than making frequent deposits of cash into her very own bank account. Just don't let her forget to earmark 10 percent of her earnings for her Secret 10.

© Concept/author David Johnston, "The Amazing Mister J–Magician" (www.misterj.ca). Illustrator: Mike Holmes.

Another comic by David Johnston, this one drawn after he read my first book, *The Cold Hard Truth: On Business, Money & Life*. My kids loved the comic and wondered if he could illustrate every chapter this way.

Age 12
Financial Planner Day

Hopefully, by age 12, your child's socked away some money. Every little deposit adds up, so her account should be growing. She's still setting aside 10 percent of everything she earns—and now that she's a petulant preteen, she probably delights in keeping her Secret 10 a secret. Assuming she does have that Secret 10, you're going to help her grow it.

For her 12th birthday, you're taking your daughter to meet your financial planner. This can be a more traditional planner, or the broker who oversees your investment portfolio. If you've got one of each, take her to both. Your daughter most likely will have a cursory understanding of the stock market from school. By seventh grade, most students have received a rudimentary lesson or two, depending on how cool their math teacher is. Maybe your kid has been lucky and has even had a chance to do some investment role play. But your advisor will be able to show her actual numbers: the gains on *your* investments. That's right. You're opening the books for your child to see—in real terms—what you have for your future.

Perhaps you want to leave it at that: showing your child your portfolio and explaining your investment philosophy. Which, if you were paying attention, should be: *never invest in a security or stock that doesn't pay a dividend or interest, and spend the interest, never the principal.*

I'm betting that, once your child sees the way your money is growing, she's going to want in. That's what happened with Trevor. I made him put 10 percent of every cent he earned into a separate account (in my trust until he turns 18), and now he's investing online. A few months ago, he asked me about dividends and interest, so I've been teaching him about dividend-paying stock. I give him advice about what to buy, advice he can take or leave, and we invest in stocks together. His first purchase was one of the O'Leary mutual funds and some Canadian bank stocks. He loves the stock market because he understands how to use it to his advantage—and he's making money now, too.

Age 13
Family Service Day

For this birthday celebration, you're going to put a twist on the money lessons you've been teaching your child all these years. Remember how I said I don't believe in little pink piggy banks because they teach kids to be selfish hoarders? This lesson is all the more important once your child starts high school, because it can be very tempting to want to compete with other kids who have "cooler" stuff. Ask any 13-year-old: It's tough being a teenager. You want so much to fit in! But trying to keep up with the Joneses only reinforces the idea that life is all about buying into brands instead of financial prudence. So this year, you're going to teach your 13-year-old an important lesson: Being a financially literate adult isn't only about what you can get. It's also about what you give.

That giving can take several forms. If your family has favorite charities, put your daughter in charge of this year's annual contribution. If you have a history of volunteering, dedicate a Family Service Day. Is there a particular organization with a mission statement that your teen thinks is really cool? Put her in charge of doing the research and setting it all up. She's old enough now to surf the web for worthwhile nonprofits, and she's more than capable of picking up the phone and scheduling a day of service. Ideally, she should choose something that the whole family can do together, whether it's volunteering in a soup kitchen, cleaning litter out of a river or planting trees. Remember, you're demonstrating good money karma. You'll get back what you put in.

If volunteering isn't your thing, here's another option: plan a Phase-Two Vacation—a vacation you go on with the whole family (not the romantic two-person getaway of yesteryear). You can even include your relatives, if you're up for it. Whenever possible, invite your siblings and their kids so your children can build deeper relationships with their cousins. Group vacations can stabilize families, which can help your kids, nieces and nephews later in life if they get into trouble. These early experiences form an irreplaceable community and a web-like system of support. Most kids don't care about their extended family when they're teenagers, but they'll really start to value them later in life.

You don't have to plan an extravagant sojourn to Maui for your son or daughter's 13th birthday—in fact I'd advise against it. The whole point is to remind them they are *not* the center of the universe. You don't even have to go far; you could just as easily have your child invite some people over for a backyard BBQ.

Age 14
The DIY Birthday
The day your child turns 14, you're going to hand over the reins. Let her plan her own birthday party. Set a fair budget and give her license to do anything she wants (within reason), as long as it doesn't violate the parameters you've set or the law. If she decides to go all out—say, she wants to rent a party boat and take all her

friends out on the lake—tell her that she's responsible for any costs that go over budget. If she's been working and saving for the last few years, she'll have access to her own funds, and if she insists on having a big bash, then she'll need to front the extra cash herself.

A lot of 14-year-olds won't respond kindly to having to pay for their own birthday party. But *your* 14-year-old is different, right? You've spent the last 10 years teaching her how to save and invest and be fiscally responsible instead of thinking of you as her personal wallet. She's been juggling odd jobs for years, socking her money away in her own savings and investment accounts (and monitoring them closely). She's growing her Secret 10 in stocks and securities that pay dividends and interest. She knows *exactly* how much money she has, and exactly how much she can afford to spend.

My kids have often opted for low-key birthday celebrations. Trevor loves steak, so we'll take a couple of his closest friends and head to a local steakhouse. Savannah loves Thai food, so she'll invite some friends over and we'll order takeout. Some of the best birthday memories at our house have been simple, inexpensive affairs. Who knows? Maybe your child will decide to blow a big chunk of change on her DIY birthday. But maybe— just maybe—she'll decide that boring ol' Mom and Dad turned out to be right: it's better to save than to spend, and having a healthy relationship with money is ultimately way more fun than blowing it on cheap thrills.

Congratulations! You've just given your child a 10-year MBA— and you didn't have to spend thousands of dollars on an advanced degree.

Money Mistake: *You Need Time to Instill Values*
The Fix: *Start a Sunday Family Dinner Tradition*

With all this emphasis on financial literacy, you might think I'm saying money is the only thing with true value. That couldn't be further from the truth. Look at the title of this chapter: Give Your Kids an MBA. Money is just the mortar. The time you spend with your kids is invaluable, worth far more than dollars.

Years ago, my wife and I started a family tradition: no matter what else was going on, we agreed to sit down together at least one night a week for a family dinner. Sunday evening worked best; I was home from work and the kids weren't running out the door to a soccer game or a party. At these Sunday dinners, we'd talk about what had happened during the previous week, sharing news and offering support. It was a time to talk about what was going on in our lives and to truly listen to one another. Linda and I learned a long time ago that the best way to get our kids to open up was if we opened up first. The minute you sit your kids down and say, "Tell us about your week," it's game over. Instead, Linda and I would talk very candidly about our own struggles—the email Linda sent out that no one responded to, the tough decision I had to make at work. Sunday-night dinners were a chance for us to share our own experiences and to invite our kids to share theirs. In our household, those evenings were sacrosanct.

As my kids grew older, they began to ask if they could invite their friends over for Sunday family dinner. The more the merrier, Linda and I felt. We encouraged Savannah and Trevor to bring people, knowing that we'd be able to share our family values in a relaxed atmosphere and have a unique window into the lives of our children. This past summer, Savannah was home and had a friend from New York University visiting for a few days. After lunch, we had a couple of drinks and started talking about dating. "Here's what I think," I said, and proceeded to share my views. Because we'd been using Sunday dinner as a forum for opinions for years, I wasn't summarily ignored! Quite the opposite, in fact. We all had a great conversation that would never have happened if we hadn't been in such an informal environment.

Just last weekend, the four of us were up at our

This is a photo from Easter dinner in 2005. I'm an advocate for getting together with family and friends as often as possible. It's occasions like these that define your life. I don't recall any elderly person ever saying to me, "I wished I had spent more time in the office." No matter how hard you work, you must find time for friends and family.

cottage in Muskoka. Linda and I were enjoying the peace and quiet, but it took all of 10 minutes for the kids to admit they'd rather have their friends with them. That weekend, we started as four and eventually became 20. We had kids from as close as Toronto to as far as New York enjoying the weekend away. Everybody wanted to be a part of it, and it was a great time for all involved. Linda and I got to talk to our children's friends, to have conversations we wouldn't have had any other way.

Be the matriarch or patriarch whenever you can, and especially on the topics of love, money and work—those topics many parents seem to avoid. Speak openly and honestly about your own mistakes, ambitions, goals and embarrassments. Humanize yourself. You'll be amazed at how quickly your kids and their cohorts will open up to you—especially if you make your home a happy, warm place where people want to be.

Linda makes a point of keeping our kitchen well stocked with homemade lasagna, spaghetti and meatballs, chicken-fried rice—all the stuff that teenagers love to eat. Trevor and his friends know that food is there for them, and they make good use of it.

If individual family members pass one another like ships in the night, hardly saying two words to each other, let alone sharing a meal, the dynasty breaks down. But families that are successful function more like clans. And make sure every member of your family has their own MBA and has absorbed lifelong lessons about responsibility, integrity and hard work. Long may your dynasty reign.

HOW TO BE AN E.T.
(ENTREPRENEUR IN TRAINING)

You don't have to invent a new product or launch a million-dollar start-up to be an E.T.. Some of the successful kids I know worked with what they had. Here are three examples of E.T.s who were making money before they could even drive—and I'm proud to say two of them are O'Learys!

1. **The baker by boat.** When Savannah was 14, she got a job at the bakery in Muskoka. She loved baking, so it was a great way to do something she enjoyed and actually get paid for it. Every morning she got up at 5:30 A.M., when the rest of us were still asleep, and took herself to the bakery. She couldn't drive yet, so she used our old Boston Whaler and went down the lake by boat! Savannah worked at that bakery for four summers, never missing a single morning. While other teenagers were out partying until 2 and 3 A.M., Savannah was in bed by a reasonable hour. Talk about making sacrifices!

2. **The camp counselor extraordinaire.** When he was 11, Trevor started babysitting for a friend of ours with young kids. He was a natural, and before long he was getting requests from other parents to babysit their kids, too. To meet demand, Trevor designed a summer program for half a dozen six-year-olds. Their parents would drop them off each morning and he would entertain them all day. He planned all sorts of activities, including soccer, gymnastics, Lego-building contests, arts and crafts, and full-fledged scavenger hunts. Trevor put a lot into this, and the kids had a blast.

3. **The garage sale profiteer.** A few summers back, one of Trevor's friends, Emma, got really bored and decided to have a garage sale. But instead of just selling her own stuff, she devised a plan to expand her profit margins. Emma went door to door and asked all of her neighbors if they had anything they'd like to sell. All they had to do was leave their goods on their front porch the morning of the sale and Emma would collect, price and sell it. "You keep 90 percent," Emma explained. "I'll take a 10 percent commission." The neighbors were thrilled—they didn't have to raise a finger and were getting most of the profits. Emma ended up collecting goods from eight different neighbors—clothes, electronics and old records—and she was able to sell some of it at a decent markup. Her 10 percent commission ended up netting Emma a solid 300 bucks!

CHAPTER 8

KIDS: GET A JOB!

About a year ago, I discovered my son had an extraordinary talent. I'd just gotten home from a *Shark Tank* shoot in Los Angeles after a long, grueling week. I was relaxing with my wife downstairs, about to enjoy a nice glass of O'Leary wine, when the whole house started to shake. The bass-pounding was so brutal I thought the ceiling was about to come down on our heads.

"What is that noise?" I asked.

Linda smiled. "Trevor!" she shouted.

We both knew our 15-year-old son liked listening to his electronic music, but by the time I got to the upstairs landing, the *boom taka taka boom taka taka* was deafening. When I pounded on Trevor's bedroom door, I could feel vibrations in my skull.

"Come in!" he yelled, and I stepped inside.

I was about to tell him to turn his horrible music off when I noticed Trevor wasn't at his stereo. He was sitting in front of two computer screens, both filled with lines of complex coding. He was bent over the keyboard, furiously typing away, as new codes appeared onscreen.

"What on earth are you doing?"

"Composing!"

And that's when I realized he wasn't just listening to this stuff; he was *writing* it.

I signaled for him to turn the volume down and take off his headphones. He obliged.

"Hey, Dad," he said, business as usual. "What's up?"

I could have started in on him about how his racket was giving the entire household a headache, but something in me knew to hold off. "Will you explain to me what you're doing?"

"Sure. Have a seat," Trevor said.

Over the next half-hour, my son walked me through some incredible software and taught me a little about the very complex authoring systems on his computer—the kind producers use to record bands.

"Want to listen?" he asked. He slipped his headphones over my ears. Once the volume was set at a rational level, I was absolutely astonished by what I heard. Trevor had laid down tracks on the piano and then modified them, downloading voices from the Internet, as well as sound bites he recorded himself. After a few minutes of listening to his composition, I could tell he had some genuine talent. I can't take any credit—my son surpassed me on the guitar years ago. He can pick up any instrument, from piano to trombone, and he just gets it. Linda's father has won all sorts of awards for choral arrangements, so Trevor must have gotten his musical genius from his mother's side.

It didn't take me long to conclude that Trevor had gotten very advanced with this electronic stuff. He was tuned in to the DJ culture around the world, and that's the sort of music he was creating—music young people could dance to.

© Matt Barnes.

Music has always been a huge part of my life. I've always loved playing the guitar (like the Gibson Les Paul seen here). This passion for music is something I've passed on to my children, especially my son, Trevor. You have to find time in your life for your passions. With instruments as beautiful as these, who wouldn't want to jam every now and then?

"I have a track called 'Orangutan,'" Trevor told me. "I've sampled orangutan screams from the jungle and made them into a music track for clubs."

"Really?"

"Yeah. Would you tweet it for me?"

Oh no, I was thinking. My son wants me to use my hard-earned fan base and tweet monkey noises to them. "You want me to do what?"

"Dad, you've got like a billion followers on Twitter."

"Let me hear the track." I listened, and again, my son blew me away. The track was enthralling and intense, musically advanced and inventive.

"This is amazing, Trevor," I said. "I'll do it. I'll tweet it." And I did. And that's when things went nuts. Suddenly, Trevor was getting all kinds of web traffic thanks to the tweet. A major producer from Atlanta contacted him by email and said, "I heard 'Orangutan.' Can you send me a mash of your tracks?" (A mash, I've since learned, is when you put your tracks in order, as if you were doing a club date.)

"Fantastic!" the producer said when he heard the mash. "When can I book you?" He assumed Trevor was a 20-something DJ looking for a gig!

Trevor started getting FedEx packages from Atlanta full of hats, shirts and jackets. "I'm going to sponsor you, and this is how we brand you," the producer told him. "I want you to start taking images and videos of yourself wearing these clothes." That's when I called Daymond John from *Shark Tank*. Daymond's very involved in music and knows his stuff.

"Is this guy for real?" I asked.

"He's legit, Kevin," Daymond reassured me. "He's a major player—he works with all the big DJs around the world. But your son's 15. Once you plunge him into this culture, there's no turning back."

Linda and I discussed it. On one hand, Trevor had an opportunity to monetize his interest, to learn about entrepreneurship, and maybe even launch a lucrative career and make some serious money. On the other, he was still just a kid! Club culture is fueled by alcohol and illicit drugs, and my wife and I don't endorse that lifestyle. The producer hinted that if Trevor's career took off, he'd have to quit school, and neither Linda nor I was up for that. "Absolutely not," she said. "He's going to finish school, and he can do this as a hobby."

So the three of us came to a mutual decision: we said no to the guy from Atlanta. Meanwhile, Trevor and I released a few more tracks on Twitter. Club owners around Toronto started calling him up, offering to pay him to do gigs. We established some ground rules. Trevor could take the DJ gigs under two conditions: never on a school night, and only if it didn't interfere with his homework. He agreed. But before he could start spinning locally, he needed some equipment. You've got to bring your own laptop and something called a tracker system to the club, and it's not cheap, I learned—a tracker system alone costs around $1,000. When Trevor asked if he could borrow $1,000 to make the purchase, I said, "Nope. You're going to have to use your own money." He was less than thrilled with this response.

If you think history is repeating itself, you're right. In my second book, I talked about the stereo system I just had to have when I was 17—the one I blew $1,700 on for a down payment before making the stupid decision to put the remaining $1,800 on credit. That number seemed totally manageable when I had a job, less so after I was laid off. I would have been paying that $1,800 off at 16 percent interest, compounded monthly, for *years* if my brother Shane hadn't bailed me out. Now, 40 years later, here was my son wanting me to finance his own fancy electronic equipment. I suddenly understood my stepfather, George, in a way I never had before.

Trevor, being only 15, didn't have a credit card, but he did have a savings account. For the previous two summers, he had worked cleaning boats—a demanding job in the hot sun, but ultimately worth it at $11 an hour. He had saved close to $1,000. The way it works in our house is like this: if you want to drive, you're responsible for all the associated fees—driver's education courses, procuring a license, and—if you're hell-bent on having your own wheels—buying a car. My kids also have to pay for their own insurance. So Trevor had saved this thousand dollars thinking about getting his license. But now he was faced with a conundrum: buying the tracker system would completely decimate his account and he wouldn't be able to start driving lessons.

"C'mon, Dad," he begged. "Just a little loan?"

You might think I'm heartless, but I practice what I preach. The money lessons we'd spent the last 15 years drilling into our

I refused to fund the purchase of my son's DJ equipment. It reminded me of the mistake I had made decades earlier, going into debt by purchasing stereo equipment. My refusal did not deter him. He used the money he made working in the summer as a boat cleaner to buy it. It cost thousands, but he recouped it all and then some by getting paid DJing gigs. Linda worries that he does not get enough sleep at night to be alert in school, but he keeps his marks up and finds time to write music. You can hear his work at trevoroleary.com.

son's head were finally being called to account. If I backed down now and became the fairy godfather, Trevor would have learned that it was all just a game and that I'd bail him out of any future money problems he'd come to have. And there was no way I wanted a son of mine to think that.

To Trevor's credit, he didn't make a spur-of-the-moment decision. He spent a couple months debating whether he should buy that tracker system and start his new small business. Then he did a little bit of research. He started going online, trying to figure out how to get the best deal on a system. In the end, he decided to buy certain components secondhand and other pieces new. He assembled them himself into a complete kit. Then he booked his first gig. It was a huge hit. The club went nuts—they loved his music! Now he's getting paid $150 a night for his gigs. He sticks $15 into his Secret 10 account after every gig, and his accounts are starting to grow. It's turning out to be a nice money-maker for him. Yes, he wiped out his savings to buy the necessary equipment—but he made it back within the first month. That's not entirely careless spending; it was a good investment.

Money Mistake: *Your Kids Think They Don't Have to Work*
The Fix: *Help Your Teenager Find a Job*

A spoiled, pampered kid isn't helping anyone—including him- or herself. Your children need a job as soon as they're old enough to work. Even young teenagers should find ways to be employed (part time, of course, and not in a way that interferes with school). Every job will give your kid a new experience and perspective, both the good and the bad.

In my teens and early 20s, I did many backbreaking jobs that made me appreciate the value of hard-earned cash and a well-chosen career. Perhaps it comes as a surprise to you that I'm no stranger to manual labor. The summer I turned 17, I got hired by a logging company to go out into the wilderness and replant trees where the logging company had hacked them down the year before. I'd walk down a row with a shovel, stuff a seedling into a hole, push down the earth around it and move on to the next one . . . hour after hour. It was strenuous work. We carried our quota of trees on our backs, the blazing sun beating down on us and the mosquitoes and blackflies eating us alive. Some guys wore thick mosquito nets, which made the work even hotter. We were paid by the tree, which meant you could only make a lot of money if you were agile and exact. It also meant the less-honest workers tried to cheat the system. I watched guys try to plant two or five trees at once to get rid of their seedlings and get paid for greater output. Of course, the managers were hip to all the scams. If they saw that you'd planted two trees in a hole, you got one free pass, in case it was an accident. If they caught you doing it again, you were outta there.

I learned plenty of life lessons at that job. I learned if I wasn't quick and competitive, I wouldn't make a lot of cash. I also learned that cheating is no way to get ahead. I made close to $5,000 that summer. For a kid, that was pretty good. But I didn't go back the next summer. There are some jobs that are just too taxing—even for 5,000 bucks.

The next summer, I opened up the Saturday-morning paper and saw the following ad: "Bricklayer needed. Must have previous experience. $12/hr." Twelve dollars an hour! Wow! (This was in the 1970s, and I was still a teen, so this sounded great to me.) There was only one problem: I had never so much as touched a brick in my life. So what did I do? I lied and said I had previous experience (never, ever a good idea). I showed up on the first day without the faintest idea of how to do anything. I couldn't even mix my own mortar, let alone put it on a trowel and lay down a brick. And these weren't the small bricks you see in nice suburban houses. These were gigantic cinderblocks for industrial buildings. I was in over my head.

Luckily for me, the foreman decided to let me stay, despite my now-obvious lies about being experienced. For the first week, he demoted me from "bricklayer" to "cinderblock carrier" and paid me a lot less. (See? Lying didn't pay off.) I'd lug bricks back and forth between the men on-site who actually knew what they were doing. During the foreman's lunch break, he took it upon himself to train me in the art of laying bricks. After one week, I picked up the basic skill set. After two weeks, my walls were mostly straight. I can't tell you how many shirts I ruined on the job. It was hard work building walls made of 30-pound bricks. The sun was beating down on me every hour of every day, and I had to take salt pills to stay hydrated. A couple of the guys on my team were hospitalized for heat stroke. At the end of the day, I was so exhausted I could hardly walk straight. I don't think I've ever slept as well as I did after a day of bricklaying. I laid bricks for the rest of the summer and came back the next summer, too, because by then I wasn't lying about having previous experience.

And those weren't even the worst jobs I've done! I spent one summer hanging off the side of a building, strapped into a harness, stripping the plywood off cement after it had solidified. There was debris flying around up there—sharp nails and pieces of drywall. It was insanely dangerous, which is why it paid so well. But by far the worst job I ever had was making bumpers for cars. I stood at a giant machine that ran 24/7. My job, hour after painful hour, was to take a strip of metal, place it on the line, pull my hands away, hit two red buttons simultaneously and—*boom*—the massive machine would clamp down on the metal, pressing it into a bumper in one swift stroke. I'd do this over and over and over again. Every bumper meant more money in the bank.

But then things started to get weird. I was terrified of having an accident. What if I didn't lift my hands in time? What if the safety tethers fastened to them didn't work? What if my hands got squashed into a bumper-shaped mash? What would become of me then? But when I raised my concerns with the foreman, he assured me that the machine would never clamp down without my hands being withdrawn through the safety tethers, and that the whole reason I had to hit two buttons simultaneously was to ensure that the machine would only work once my hands were safely away from the press.

I felt better after hearing that. Then, on my third day in the shop, I wasn't *anywhere near* the two buttons when the machine went *boom*. All by itself. I saw it with my own two eyes! I went to the foreman and told him what had happened.

"Nah, kid," he said. "You're just daydreaming. It's mind-numbing work. People hallucinate all the time," he told me. "The monotony is making you see things."

"Sir, I'm sorry to have to tell you this, but I am not seeing things. There's something wrong with that machine."

No matter what I said, he refused to believe me.

I saw the same thing happen three more times and complained at every instance, only to get the same shoulder-shrugging response. And that's when I had to take matters into my own hands — before I lost them. In my mind, I was thinking how much money my hands were worth to me, and no matter what dollar value I put on them, nothing was enough. That's when I decided, "Nope! Can't do this," and quit on the spot.

That was the worst job I ever had. I was lucky, for sure, that I never had a serious accident in any of these jobs, but apart from that, I'm also grateful to have learned the immensely valuable lesson about working hard for every penny and making sure that the work I did was valued properly. These experiences gave me a very clear sense of the kind of work I found fulfilling — and the kind I didn't. They motivated me to do something with my life where I would be safe and financially rewarded.

Money Mistake: *You're Still Funding Your Teenager's Lifestyle*
The Fix: *No Free Tickets!*

One surefire way to nudge your teenagers into the workforce is by setting firm boundaries on what you will and will not pay for. Agree to pay for room, board and education — and then draw a line in the sand.

Last year, before Trevor's DJ business took off, I took him with me on a flight to Europe. As usual, I bought myself a first-class ticket. At this point in my life, I think I've earned the right to a more comfortable travel experience. But Trevor got a seat in economy. He wasn't happy about it. "Why do I have to sit all cramped up in the back?" he whined. "You always get the bigger screen and the better food!"

"Son, you can sit in the front any time you like—provided you pay for it."

"But I don't have that kind of cash!"

"Trevor," I said, "that's your problem, not mine."

When Linda travels with me, she likes the whole family to sit together, even though we could save 10 grand by putting Trevor and Savannah in the back. Because she's much more of a softie than I am, she'll say, "I can't do that." And I say, "Well, I can." And I have. I've bought my kids economy-class seats dozens of times.

Call me a monster if you want, but let's face it: it's not like I don't know where the kids are. I save a ton of money every time I do this, but that's not the real reason I make this choice. At 16, my son is making the connection between money and personal freedom. I think that's the greatest gift I've ever given him: to help him see that connection. And I constantly reinforce it by doing Mean Dad things like making him sit in those crappy economy seats. Financial literacy is not about hoarding cash. It's about recognizing and respecting money for its *true* value: the personal freedom it allows you to enjoy.

SIX SAFE SUMMER JOBS FOR TEENAGERS

Don't worry: I'm not going to suggest you send your kid off to work on a bumper-making machine line or strapped into a dangerous harness, washing windows high in the city skies. Here are some safe summer jobs that can actually be quite lucrative. Encourage your teen to start the job search early. Many places recruit their summer staff as early as January.

1. **Golf caddy.** There's a fortune waiting at the neighborhood golf course. Most caddies earn between $50 and $100 a bag. Though your child will have to be on his or her feet four to five hours at a time, the work is fairly straightforward: carrying bags, cleaning balls and repairing divots. If your son or daughter is an extra-eager caddy who is willing to work a double shift, he or she could rake in as much as $200 to $300 a day.

2. **Summer entrepreneur.** If your family lives in Ontario, your children have access to a very cool program called Summer Company. The program is designed to help young entrepreneurs between the ages of 15 and 29 start a summer business. Your son or daughter can apply for a $3,000 grant, and if they are selected, they will receive the start-up money as well as advice and mentorship from local business leaders. If your child has expressed an interest in owning a small business someday, this is the perfect way to get them started. Go to the website for more info: www.ontario.ca/business-and-economy/start-summer-business-students

3. **Product merchandiser.** You know those smiling young people handing out samples at the grocery store? Those are product

merchandisers. They also restock the shelves and take inventory. It's a good, safe job with the perk of being indoors during the steamy summer months. And it usually pays slightly over minimum wage, averaging around $12.50 an hour.

4. **Camp counselor/lifeguard.** What's summer without summer camp? If your teen goes to work every day in a fun, vibrant environment, he or she will be much more excited to get out of bed in the morning. The pay isn't usually great, but the community of people can make up for it. And we all know that being a lifeguard carries plenty of cultural cachet (not to mention a nice tan by the end of the summer). The Canadian Red Cross Lifeguard program allows kids to be certified at age 15. Talk about a great way to teach your teenagers about responsibility: they'll actually be safeguarding people's lives.

5. **Junior park ranger.** Parks Canada (www.pc.gc.ca) offers over 1,000 student jobs across the nation. They typically run from May to September and give students opportunities to work in resource conservation, visitor services, heritage preservation and waterways. Your teenager will get valuable experience and a great boost to the résumé. Linda spent one summer on the Trent-Severn Waterway, Lock 44. She greeted the boats as they came in, took their lines, tied them up and sold them a pass to go through the locks for the day. She got to spend all day on the water, talking to boaters, and she absolutely loved it. The first summer she applied, she didn't get the job, so encourage your teens to be persistent; if they don't get it the first time, urge them to apply again.

6. **Caregiver.** Does your teenager have a passion for helping the elderly? Consider finding a way to monetize his or her skills. He or she will need to be up-front about their age and lack of professional training, but there are plenty of positions for non-medical assistants. This

could take the form of helping an elderly neighbor or relative, or offering services to a seniors' facility. Many centers are always on the lookout for young, bright people to come in and interact with their residents.

CHAPTER 9

SINGLE PARENTS, BLENDED FAMILIES, ADOPTED KIDS: A FINANCIAL STRATEGY

Michelle Obama once referred to herself on national television as a single mom. It was an unintentional gaffe. Later, the First Lady clarified: "Sometimes, when you've got a husband who is president, it can feel a little single," she said. "But he's there."

I can understand where she's coming from. My mother, Georgette, was a single parent long before my father left. Terry was an old-style Irishman: he was out with his buddies, drinking and living a wild life. He was never home with his family. My mother had to be responsible not just for herself but also for her wayward husband and two young children. She wasn't getting much in the way of support from Terry—financially or emotionally.

It's an all-too-familiar story: the workaholic man pursuing success, often at the expense of time spent with his family. Or the professional woman climbing the corporate ladder, working day and night while her husband stays at home with the kids. In either scenario, the stay-at-home partner is essentially a single parent raising the kids.

To be honest, I spent several years MIA myself. When I was growing my first business, The Learning Company, my long-term goal was to provide for my family, so I spent the majority of every day working. I missed a lot of magical moments when my kids were young. It was a huge sacrifice, and I like to think it paid off with the family dynasty I've been able to offer—but I know for a fact that Linda often felt like a single parent during those early years.

If you're a single parent, I want to say right now that I have tremendous respect for you. You are doing the most important job in the world, and you are doing it alone. Hats off to you for the incredible amount of time, effort and love you pour into your work every day.

You're not alone. According to Statistics Canada, single-parent households have been on the rise for the last four decades. In 2011, 16 percent of families were classified as "lone-parent families." Eight out of 10 times, the lone parent is female. Sadly, homes headed by a single mother are at a significant economic disadvantage compared to married couples and common-law partners. The difference in income is striking. In 2011, the median after-tax income for two-parent families with children was $83,600, whereas the median after-tax income for female *lone*-parent families was $39,900. This is tragic because it means the youngest members of society—children—suffer most. Only 5.9 percent of children being raised by two parents are living in low income. Compare that to 23 percent of children being raised by a single parent.

You may not be a typical single parent. Maybe your spouse passed away and you were forced into single parenthood against your will. Maybe you're married to a workaholic who's never around to help with the kids or the house. I don't know your personal situation or your relationship history. The one thing I do know is that if you're a single parent, the rules may be harder, but they do apply.

Money Mistake: *You Spoil Your Kids Out of Guilt*
The Fix: *Instill a Sense of Autonomy Instead*

When you're raising children alone, there is often a temptation to make up for the absence of the other parent. Not only is this financially unsustainable, it's not helping your kids. Study after study has shown that when parents constantly hover over their children, giving them everything they ask for (and plenty of stuff besides), those children grow up to be less-confident adults. They never learn to function independently of their parents; instead of self-sufficiency, they inherit a sense of entitlement, expecting the world to cater to their every whim. I used to find it baffling how so many of my divorced friends' kids displayed a staggering sense of entitlement. Then I realized it was their own guilt-ridden parents who had created the little monsters.

Instead of spoiling your children with iPods and smart phones and laptops, enlist their help. You're working twice as hard to keep the family afloat—they can contribute, too, by completing household chores and other assigned tasks. They should be able to take care of some things themselves, from basic hygiene to homework to keeping their rooms tidy. Each member of the family must learn to pull his or her own weight.

It's a peculiar symptom of modern times that our children have become more infantilized. I can't tell you how many single mothers I've met who are juggling two and three jobs to make ends meet, and their kids can't be bothered to stop playing Xbox games long enough to come and help them put away the groceries they just worked hard to buy. This problem seems to be particularly problematic in North America, where kids enjoy a protracted childhood — so protracted that 30-year-olds think it's okay to move back home. In some cultures, this kind of dependence is simply unacceptable.

Take the Matsigenka people of the Amazon, a tribe of about 12,000 people living in Peru. Matsigenka toddlers use machetes to cut wood for kindling and prepare their own food over an open fire. Six- and seven-year-olds accompany their parents on hunting trips and help prepare meals in the kitchen. By puberty, the children of the Matsigenka have learned essential survival skills. Not only that — they can use their skills to help the whole tribe survive.

It's time you started thinking of your family as a tribe. This is especially true if you're a single parent. Your tribe may be small, but that doesn't make it less of one. The more

My mother, Georgette, at Easter making pastries with her good friend Mary Lenas and others. Georgette believed the simplest family activities could engage children and their friends in a way that forms bonds. You don't see video games here, just children rolling dough.

161

you can foster autonomy and competence in your kids, the stronger your tribe will be.

When you're alone with your kids, focus on spending quality time, not quality cash. I once knew a single mom who didn't have much money for Christmas presents. On Christmas Eve, she took her four kids to the dollar store and gave them each $5 to buy presents for each other. Guess what? They had a blast. That mom spent a grand total of $25 on Christmas presents. And yet her four kids, now adults, remember that year fondly, because they had to come together in the trenches of poverty to make the most of it. Their mother had done an excellent job of teaching them to be grateful for what they had: namely, each other.

Money Mistake: *Getting Remarried Is Too Expensive*
The Fix: *Wrong! Consider the Long-Term Financial Benefits*

As single-parent households are on the rise, so, too, are blended families. The two-parents-and-three-kids formula of the 1950s is no longer the norm. Today's families are more complex, many formed by second and third marriages. Statistics Canada has always provided data for "intact families"—families with no incidence of divorce or remarriage—but for the first time in 2011, the census also measured the number of stepfamilies in the country. Out of 3.7 million two-parent families with children, 12.6 percent are stepfamilies. One out of every 10 children in Canada is now a member of a blended family.

Stepfamilies bring their own challenges, but I believe it's better to get remarried than to live out the rest of your days alone. Why? Because remarriage is the single best decision you can make for your financial dynasty—provided you've learned from the first and that this one will last.

Getting remarried after a period of single parenthood can ease your financial responsibilities and put more money in the bank. Statistically, there is *no significant difference* between the family income of parents in stepfamilies and those in intact families. If you stay single, however, the odds are stacked against you: 49 percent of lone-parent families have a household income of less than $50,000. Compare that to just 16 percent of stepfamilies. When you look at the numbers, stepfamilies actually perform quite well, with 41 percent netting an annual income of $100,000 or more. But only 9 *percent* of lone-parent families ever make it to 100 k. As you can see from the following table, the cost of remaining single is just too high.

HOUSEHOLD INCOME OF INTACT, STEP- AND LONE-PARENT FAMILIES

	INTACT (FIRST MARRIAGE)	STEP-FAMILY	LONE PARENT
Household Income			
Less than $50,000	13%	16%	49%
$50,000 to $79,999	19%	21%	20%
$80,000 to $99,999	13%	12%	7%
$100,000 to $149,999	25%	24%	7%
$150,000 or more	19%	17%	2%
Not stated	11%	9%	15%

Source: Statistics Canada, General Social Survey, 2011.

Of course, marrying someone with children from a prior union can incur hidden expenses. I've got a friend who has been divorced three times. He has two adopted sons, both in their 20s. He recently fell in love with a beautiful Colombian woman with a 14-year-old son. She's 20 years his junior, but she's crazy about him. When he asked her to marry him, she said yes. It's a real-life *Modern Family*.

My friend's adult children went nuts when they heard the news. "We don't need a little brother, Dad!" they said. "He just got a cut of the family inheritance." Talk about the kids of divorce showing a sense of entitlement!

But my friend went ahead and married his real-life Sofía Vergara. He didn't want to live the rest of his life alone; he wanted a mate. And his mate needed some stability for her son. Meanwhile, my friend is 62 and figures he has only about a decade left of good health. After three hard divorces, he just wants to be happy. But in order to move forward, I advised him to think long and hard about how to stabilize his family dynasty. His two grown sons clearly have expectations, and now he has a new wife and teenager to support. (The solution, by the way, is to provide for the 14-year-old with some kind of endowment or trust. That way, my friend protects his children's inheritance while still providing stability for his new stepson. Everybody wins. Everything is clear.)

Money Mistake: *You Think You Can't Afford to Adopt*
The Fix: *Treat the Initial Cost as a One-Time Payment*

If you can't conceive, I have great news for you: you can still create the family you've always wanted. I have friends who have adopted multiple kids and love their families to pieces. Their children make their lives rich, bringing all the joys and blessings of parenthood— and all the challenges and financial burdens, too.

Deciding to adopt is a big financial decision. Most private domestic adoptions will set you back between $15,000 and $25,000 for a child born in Canada, and international adoptions (for a child born in the U.S. or another country) can range from $25,000 to over $50,000.

But if your heart is set on adopting, don't let those numbers scare you more than they should. It's really the same cost as having a baby: it's just that you pay more up front. With a biological child, that $25,000 is spread out over the pregnancy and the first year of the baby's life. If your budget simply won't allow that one-time payment, consider a public domestic adoption, where there is typically no fee. Even in the worst-case scenario, you won't be paying more than $3,000. Fair warning: the waiting period for a healthy newborn is extremely long. Many children available for public adoption are special-needs children. If this is something you're passionate about, by all means, go for it. But if you don't have the financial and emotional resources to take this on, consider other options.

Incidentally, I'm soon to be an adopted child myself. George, the man who has acted as my father for the last 50 years, is in the process of adopting me so that the Swiss government will formally recognize me as his son. I just celebrated my 59th birthday, making me the oldest man in the history of Ontario to be adopted. How's that for eternal youth?

TEN WAYS TO MINIMIZE KID-SPENDING MADNESS

Whether you're a single mom on a tight budget or a stepdad trying to feed his tribe, there are plenty of ways to save money with kids in the house. Make it into a game—one the whole family can play. Draw up a chart, put it up in the kitchen and have your kids mark down all the times they save a buck or two.

Here are some tried-and-true ways to cut down on costs. Remember: every penny counts.

1. **Don't cut corners, cut hair**. When your kids are young, they don't care about having the hippest new 'do—they just need the hair out of their eyes. So be the barber for your family and you'll save money. Take a few classes or watch a YouTube video. Bonus: you'll score a little extra bonding time when your kid's in the barber chair.

2. **Pick and choose your name brands.** When you go grocery shopping or to the pharmacy, you'll see a lot of name brands at a hefty markup. But more often than not, the store brand has *exactly* the same ingredients for half the price. Decide on the stuff you won't compromise on—for us, it's brand-name ketchup and paper towels—and then buy the store brand of everything else.

3. **Put toys on rotation.** If you're like most North American families, your living room, den and child's bedroom are clogged with toys. But no kid needs that many all the time—and wow, are those things expensive! When Savannah was small, Linda would sock some of her toys away and then, instead of buying her the new things when

she got bored, Linda would take out the stashed ones. Savannah was delighted—it was like she had brand new toys. I was delighted, too: I didn't have to buy a thing. Bonus: you'll cut down on clutter and have fewer toys to trip on in the middle of the night.

4. **Minimize the meat.** The most expensive items on any grocery list are the meat products—beef, chicken, pork, fish. But you don't have to have meat at every meal. Eat like a vegetarian every once in a while, subbing in potatoes, mushrooms, eggplants and other vegetables instead of pricey meat. Bonus: your arteries will thank you.

5. **Use the barter system**. We have a family friend who's a piano teacher and a single mom. Her kids are grown now, but when they were school-aged, she always managed to get her kids into private schools. How'd she afford it? She offered her services in exchange for tuition. She gave piano lessons and taught music classes. The barter system is still alive and well—you just have to trade something that other people want. Bonus: you'll be more involved in your community.

6. **Make their clothes last.** Kids don't need designer clothes. There is nothing more senseless than buying couture onesies for your one-year-old. Frankly, I don't think children need designer clothes at any age. Kids outgrow stuff quickly, so your goal should be to make their basic wardrobes last as long as possible. When they outgrow their blue jeans, cut them off. Voilà: now they've got jean cutoffs for the summer. Don't fall into the trap of keeping up with the Joneses when it comes to kids' wardrobes. Believe me, it's better to save the extra money and use it for something of real, lasting value—such as your children's education. Older kids can pass clothes down to their younger siblings, even across genders. Most shirts, sweaters,

and even some pants are unisex. Bonus: maybe your kids will start a new trend.

7. **Teach 'em a trade.** Anything you can teach your kids about maintenance, do it. If you don't know how to do it yourself, you can learn together. I know kids who've taught themselves basic car maintenance by watching how-to videos online—and they've saved thousands of dollars by not going to a mechanic. At the very least, your teenager should be able to change a tire and check the oil in a vehicle. One of Linda's pet peeves is when moms take their preschool daughters to get manicures and pedicures. If that kid is already getting biweekly pedicures at age five, do you know how much that's going to cost over her lifetime? And guess who your daughter thinks will pay forever— you! Instead, teach your daughter to give herself *and you* a mani- pedi. Bonus: if your kids end up getting good at changing oil or giving pedicures, they might even start a side business to rake in a little extra cash.

8. **Visit the local library.** It goes without saying that you should be checking books out rather than buying them new at the bookstore. But the library is also a great source of movie rentals—they've usually got a pretty extensive collection of DVDs. Instead of writing a check to Netflix every month or coughing up $80 to take the whole brood to a movie theater, head to your local library instead. Bonus: you won't have to keep buying new shelves to store all your books and films.

9. **Take a dip in a public pool.** Spare yourself the cost of a country club membership and swim at a public pool instead. If you're in a mountainous area, scope out the streams and lakes nearby. Bonus: you're getting exercise and spending time with the family.

10. **Seek out "Kids Eat Free" nights.** Most restaurants offer free meals to kids on a certain night of the week (usually Mondays or Tuesdays), or they may offer special child discounts between certain hours. Do your homework and find out which restaurant offers what and when. Bonus: you can treat the family to a nice dinner out at half the price.

CHAPTER 10

A LETTER TO YOUR TEENAGER, FROM UNCLE KEVIN

I know a thing or two about teenagers. I've got Trevor still living at home, and Savannah has just barely crossed the threshold into adulthood. One of the things I know about teens is that they don't always like to take advice from their parents. It doesn't matter how good the advice is—the minute you try to dispense it, they stop listening.

Interestingly, other people can give your teens advice and there is a chance they will listen. So, I'm going to make it easy for you. Uncle Kevin has a lot to say to your teenager. Hand this book over to your adolescent, because this chapter is for them.

Dear Teen,

Uncle Kevin here. Yes, that Uncle Kevin, the grumpy old geezer with no hair who you've seen on TV. Here's what you need to know: it was once the other way around! I was just like you! I had a ton of hair, but no money! Let me tell you something: the other way around is better, I assure you.

So your parents are reading a book on love and money. "Yeah?" you say. "What's that got to do with me?" I'll tell you. You are never too young to start being smart with your money. You're not in any debt—yet—unlike your parents. They're scrambling to make up for past mistakes, while you've got nothing but time on your side.

Being a teen is tough. I know; I've been there. Your less-savvy friends might blow their cash on the latest and greatest purchase—whatever that may be (and believe me: it's never the same from one week to the next). Don't make the same mistakes as them. I wish someone had told me how to be smart with my money, even when none of my friends were being smart with theirs. Sure, I've achieved the freedom that comes with having money. But I would have achieved that freedom a lot sooner if someone had shared with me what I'm about to share with you.

Read on.

Yours truly,

Uncle Kevin

At 17 I was a party animal! I didn't have a plan and I was uncertain of what to do next. I had just discovered photography and was thinking I could make a living doing that. My stepfather, George, was instrumental in getting me back on track. He convinced me to stay in school and eventually pursue a career as an entrepreneur. To this day, I am grateful for his guidance and for helping me realize I owe my children the same kind of support.

Money Mistake: *You Think You're Too Young to Establish Credit*
The Fix: *Start Building Your Credit Rating at Age 16*

If you think you have to be 18 to start building credit, think again. With rare exception, you can become an authorized user on your parents' credit card at 16. This means you'll be issued your very own card. You'll want to talk it over with them, of course, and you'll need to prove to them that you can be responsible. Think of the next two years as "credit training wheels."

Your parents are going to see every purchase you make and hold you accountable for them, and they'll know if you're making payments on time. The second you miss a payment, out come the scissors to slice up your card. Got that?

This arrangement is even better for you if your parents have good credit: your credit rating will improve by association, which will make it easier to qualify for your own separate credit card once you turn 18. Your first credit card lets the rating agencies measure your propensity to pay back your debt on time and on schedule. That's why it's so important to get one: it's how you start building your score.

Your credit score is a number between 300 and 900, where higher is better. Anything over 700 is a pretty good credit score. Every institution has slightly different requirements for what is considered "good credit," but if you keep your score above 700, you'll be safe. If you're under 500, you'll probably have trouble getting a loan. And if your score is closer to 300, no one will give you a line of credit—you're simply not worth the risk, especially for large debt obligations like a mortgage. I know that's quite a ways in the future, but it's something to consider now. Don't let mistakes you make as a teen limit your life later.

Keep in mind that even if your credit history is flawless, you won't have an excellent score for a few years because your credit age is still young. The credit card companies haven't figured you out yet; you've got to prove yourself before they hand out a first-rate score. Remember that a score represents a specific moment in time, and that's a good thing—it means you can always change your score by changing your behavior.

So how do you act responsibly once you've been added to your parents' credit card? Start small. I suggest charging minor purchases—like a tankful of gas or a meal out at a restaurant—no more than once or twice a month. Pay the total off by the due date—in full. Listen carefully: in your world, there is *no such thing as a credit card balance.* Got that? There is no way on earth you can get a two-digit return, and your savings will never pay for the interest. It's not possible. So you pay off your credit card every single month, never carrying a balance into a second month.

I'm going to lay out for you how the credit card company makes money off your bad decisions. Let's say you just *had* to have that new iPad now, even though you don't have the cash to pay for it. The Mac genius swipes your plastic and you head home the proud owner of a brand new iPad. Success, right?

Wrong. You failed to take into account that your APR (annual percentage rate) is 22 percent. That's your yearly rate of interest. If it's a nominal APR, you're paying an additional 1.83 percent every month you carry a balance (22 percent divided by 12 months). If it's an effective APR, that rate is compounded. Compounding is exactly what you want when you're saving or investing money; it's *not* what you want when you owe that money to someone else. Of course, the credit card company doesn't want you to pay attention to those numbers. Canada just passed a new law where your bill must now include the number of years it will take to pay off your bill if you pay the mere minimum every month, but good luck finding it—the print is so small you'll need a magnifying glass to read it, even with your young eyes. It's in the company's best interest to keep you in the dark about how many years you'll be in indentured servitude!

Let's say your iPad cost you an even $1,000. Your APR is 22 percent—a common enough interest rate for credit card holders today. In the following chart, I've laid out four options. Option A shows you how long it will take you to pay off that $1,000 if you make the minimum payment of $30 each month, and how much you'll end up paying in interest. Option B is how much you'll owe if you put down an additional $5 each month. Option C is if you pay the minimum plus $10. And Option D shows you the results if you pay a fixed amount: in this example, $100 each month. Look at the difference between those four options! Option D has you paying off your debt in a year. If you pay the minimum—which is what the credit card company wants you to do—they'll own your soul for the next four years and four months of your life, and worse. That iPad that you paid $1,000 for actually cost you almost $1,600. And guess what? By the time you own it outright, you're going to need a new one.

PAYING OFF CREDIT CARD DEBT:
FOUR BAD SCENARIOS

For a $1,000 Purchase with an APA of 22 percent

	OPTION A	OPTION B	OPTION C	OPTION D
	You make the minimum payment ($30/month)	You make the minimum payment plus $5/month ($35/month)	You make the minimum payment plus $10/month ($40/month)	You pay a fixed amount ($100/month)
Time to pay off your balance	4 years, 4 months	3 years, 5 months	2 years, 10 months	1 year
Interest paid	$559.61	$429.41	$349.98	$114.89
Total paid	$1,559.61	$1,429.41	$1,349.98	$1,114.89

Source: Table designed using data from Credit Card Payment Calculator, Financial Consumer Agency of Canada, 2013.

Look at those totals. That's why you must never carry a balance. It's simply not worth it. Whether they shake you down for an extra $114.89 in interest or $559.61, you've paid a huge premium on your goods.

I don't say any of this to scare you. You absolutely should and must have a credit card—it's the only way to build your credit score. I tell kids to apply for their own credit card the day they turn 18. I'm serious: go down to the bank on your birthday and fill out the paperwork. My daughter, Savannah, got a Bank of America credit card as soon as she turned 18. It took us countless hours to wade through all the paperwork and bureaucratic red tape, but it was worth it. She's spent the last three years building her credit score, and her diligence has paid off.

Your local bank will have offers from all the big companies — Visa, MasterCard, Discover, American Express. It's best to pick one company and stick with them. Do your homework and compare APRs of all the major cards; here, lower is better. Once you've made your choice, put the card in your own name — even if it means your parents will have to be co-signers for a while. By now, they trust you to use credit responsibly, so the decision to co-sign should be a no-brainer.

Most credit cards offer a zero-percent APR for an introductory period of six, 12 or 18 months. Don't abuse it. Zero percent APR does not give you free rein to use your card whenever you feel like it. Make no mistake: you're still on the hook for paying off 100 percent of your charges *by the due date*. Don't make the mistake of thinking you'll pay later. Remember what happened in 2008? How the economy collapsed and your parents were freaking out and the media were full of stories of gloom and doom? One of the big reasons for the financial crisis was that people were maxing out their credit cards and realizing only too late that they had no way to pay them off when their job situation changed for the worse. Don't let that be you.

Money Mistake: *You're Not Safe About Sex*
The Fix: *Spend $2 to Avoid Spending $250,000*

Don't worry — I'm not going to lecture you about sex, only about money. *You cannot afford the cost of an accidental pregnancy.*

Girls, you can't afford to get pregnant. Guys, you can't afford to get a girl pregnant. Earlier in this book, I talked about how much it costs to raise a kid. You're looking at $243,660 from diapers to diploma. You can't take on that kind of commitment when you're a teenager, the time in your life when you have the *least* equity.

To all the young women out there, I hate to say it, but the cost is much higher for you. The correlation between teen pregnancy and high school dropout rates is huge. If you do drop out of school, the future gets even bleaker. According to Statistics Canada, women without a high school diploma make, on average, less than $30,000 a year, putting them officially under the "low income" line.

Be safe. It doesn't cost much to take the necessary precautions. You know how much a condom costs? Less than two bucks. Now that's a great investment!

Money Mistake: *You're Living a Fast, Wild Life*
The Fix: *Slow Down Before You Pay the Price*

Being a speed demon will cost you. When I was a teenager, I had a friend who managed to get 10 speeding tickets over a one-year period. Not only did this do catastrophic damage to her driving record, it cost her over $3,000 to pay the fines and take the required drivers' safety classes. She didn't just burn rubber—she burned money and time.

If you drive with a lead foot, I strongly suggest you to find a better place for your "talents" than the open road—namely, the video game console in your home. Out of 2,227 motor vehicle fatalities in Canada in 2010, 234 were between the ages of 15 and 19. That's over

10 percent. So when I talk about "paying the price," I'm not just talking about shelling out a few thousand bucks for speeding tickets. I'm talking about paying the ultimate price: your life.

Parking tickets, though far less dangerous, are another hidden cost. In the early 1980s, I was just another irresponsible kid. At the time, I had a job downtown, so when I went to work, I always parked in the same spot on the street. I guess it wasn't technically a parking spot, because I collected over 400 parking tickets. I had an old sewing table my mother gave me, and one of the drawers was a perfect fit for the tickets. Every time I got another parking ticket, I would pop it right into that drawer and never think about it again. "They'll never catch me," I told my friends. Every once in a while, I'd change my address so they couldn't track me down. I did that for three years.

Then one day, I received a notice in the mail telling me I wasn't going to be able to renew my license. All the unpaid parking tickets sitting in that drawer had gone into a penalty phase. That was bad news, since I had to drive to work every day. I put on a suit, went downtown to the fines office and begged for mercy. Eventually, they agreed to settle. It cost me $4,500. See? I haven't always been good with money. I learned the hard way so you don't have to.

Money Mistake: *Your Drug Use Is "Recreational"*
The Fix: *You Can't Afford a Drug Addiction—Period.*

It can be easy to justify. You've got it under control, right? You're not an addict. I'm going to shoot straight with you: messing around with drugs is never worth it, for lots of reasons. But the financial impact on the rest of your life will be colossal.

179

Drugs cost money—money that could be going into your Secret 10. Then there's the cost of addiction. No one ever thinks they're going to become addicted. *No one.* That means every single addict out there was once a kid just like you, saying, "I'm not going to get hooked." And what do you know? They got hooked! I hope I don't have to tell you how devastating drug addiction can be to your future, not to mention your future relationships. Drugs erode the entire foundation of your partnership.

Look, I'm no saint. I experimented with drugs when I was young. I also saw the damage it did to the people around me. I watched a couple of close friends go off the rails at an early age. One of them got involved in dealing and ultimately went to prison. It ruined his life forever. Another guy did so many drugs that it permanently affected his personality and he became mentally unstable.

People tend to forget the indirect costs of using; you don't have to be a full-fledged addict to pay the price. Tony was a friend of mine at university, a nice enough guy who liked to smoke up occasionally. One night, Tony was driving a little too fast and got pulled over. His eyes were bloodshot, which made the officer suspicious. She opened the glove compartment and found 30 grams of marijuana in a small plastic bag. Tony was fined $1,000 and charged with minor possession. A first-time conviction can result in up to six months of jail time, so Tony got off easy with just a fine.

But the story doesn't end there. Minor possession of small amounts of marijuana is a summary offense—less serious than an indictable offense, but it still gets entered in the criminal justice system. The court kept a record of Tony's conviction, which would follow him around *for the rest of his life.* He got rejected for every credit card he applied for. He had to cancel his trip abroad because he had trouble getting a visa. A few years later, Tony moved to New York and started applying to graduate schools. Every application he filled out, he had to check the "yes" box next to "Do you have a misdemeanor on your permanent record?" When Tony didn't get into a program, he tried to enter the workforce. But every job application asked the same question. That little box seriously hurt Tony's chances of getting hired by a respectable company. He finally found an organization that was willing to overlook his past indiscretions, but he knows his salary has suffered because of it.

A criminal record is virtually impossible to expunge, and it's going to hit you right where it hurts: in the wallet. I don't care if you're having the time of your life right now; you've got to think about your future. One careless night of "fun" is all it takes to make a big mistake—one you could spend the rest of your life paying for.

Money Mistake: *You're Only Going to University to Placate Your Parents*
The Fix: *Consider a Cold Hard Cash Career*

If you've read my second book, you know I'm not one of those people who think everyone should go to university. It may not be the best choice for you—and that's perfectly okay. Better to figure that out now before your parents bankrupt themselves trying to pay for a career you can't stand.

Once upon a time, every proud mama and papa wanted their precious little cherub to grow up to be a rich doctor, lawyer or banker. Today's landscape has changed. These days it can pay to be a blue-collar worker. And I mean that literally. In the "Best Jobs in Canada" rankings for 2013, seven construction and resource-sector jobs made it into the top 50. Not just that, but "oil and gas drilling supervisor" nabbed the number one spot. The "best jobs" are ranked using Canadian data on employment and wages over a six-year span, meaning these positions are some of the best in the country in terms of salary, growth potential, job availability and future demand. The Conference Board of Canada estimates that *40 percent of all new jobs will be in the skilled trades and technology industry by 2020.*

I can't tell you how many people I've met who started on the shop floor and ended up in the chairman's suite. It doesn't always happen that way, of course, but the trades are places where upward mobility is still possible. Compare that to the business world, where it's a slow, arduous climb. "Cold hard cash" industries offer jobs with real revenue and ample employment opportunities, two things that can be hard to come by in white-collar industries. When I speak at high schools, I make a point of saying, "Look, kids—the stigma of not having a university degree is complete bull. You want an income as soon as you can get one, and you want to be able to provide for the family you'll have someday. That could mean a trade. And that's okay! In fact, it's great."

If you think a cold hard cash career might be right for you, do some research. Use the information that follows as a starting point and dig around online for more. Talk to your school counselor about what classes you could take to prepare you for trade school. Even better, talk to people who are actually working in these fields. And next time your parents give you grief about not going to university, show them the numbers. In this tenuous job market, they should rejoice that you are pursuing a sustainable career with good prospects—and the opportunity to make lots of cash.

TEN COLD HARD CASH CAREERS

All of the 10 cold hard cash careers that follow ranked among the top 50 jobs in a 2013 edition of *Canadian Business*. I've provided some basic statistics for each—the median annual salary, change in salary between 2006 and 2012, and growth in number of employees over the same six-year span. For some, I've included projected job openings for every person seeking employment in the field in 2020. You'll notice that seven of the 10 are lucrative construction and resource-sector jobs. If you think these jobs are just for men, think again. Women can do any one of these jobs; in fact, these sectors need more women. If any of the following jobs pique your interest, I suggest you drill deeper and see what you can find.

1. **Oil and gas drilling supervisor.** *Top 50 rank: #1.* I'd say it's pretty telling that this job beat out all the rest—including doctors, lawyers and bankers, with all their pompous prestige. If you're interested in a managerial position, this could be a great fit: as a supervisor, you'd be managing the personnel and running the equipment on an oil-and-gas job site. This sector has experienced phenomenal growth: *44 percent* over the last six years. The salary has gone up almost as much—39 percent since 2006—and there are expected to be a staggering *2.3 jobs* for every qualified worker in 2020. With rare exceptions, you only need a college diploma, industry training and certificates, and experience to get this job. And the median annual salary is fantastic: $74,880 in 2012.

2. **Audiologist and speech-language pathologist.** *Top 50 rank: #11.* Speech therapists are in high demand today, in light of the ever-growing numbers of children with autism and speech impediments

and the high percentage of seniors suffering from debilitating strokes that damage the language centers in the brain. As a result, this sector has experienced 29 percent growth, and the median salary was $77,813 in 2012. This job requires a master's degree, however, so be wary of the crushing burden of grad school debt.

3. **Construction manager.** *Top 50 rank: #13.* The construction industry has enjoyed almost as much growth as oil and gas drilling: there were 39 percent more employees in 2012 than there were in 2006. The mean salary is $72,800, which explains why more young men and women are setting their sights on building. You'll need a good understanding of both sides of the business—how to please both the client who hires you and the contractors you hire—because as construction manager, it will be your job to see every project through from beginning to end.

4. **Registered nurse.** *Top 50 rank: #16.* RNs will be in greater demand as people continue to live longer and longer. And nurses' salaries are going up. The median annual salary for a registered nurse in 2012 was $72,072, which is a 24 percent increase since 2006. Most provinces in Canada prefer an RN to have at least a bachelor's degree, but that isn't always the case. Quebec, for example, grants RN status to qualified college graduates. If you love helping people and want to actually make a life-or-death difference, this could be a great career for you.

5. **Dental hygienist.** *Top 50 rank: #18.* This sector has experienced a phenomenal 30 percent increase over the last six years. Hygienists today make a median salary of $69,992, and there will be a projected 1.2 job openings per person in 2020. Here's the really good news: you must complete either a bachelor program *or* a dental hygiene diploma to be licensed and registered. The

Commission on Dental Accreditation of Canada approves various programs, including many at colleges and private institutions. That means you can sidestep a pricey university degree and still make a killing by drilling.

6. **Metal-forming contractor and supervisor.** *Top 50 rank: #21.* Did you know there's a whole industry around metalworking? It shouldn't come as a surprise, considering how much metal we use in everyday life. The field encompasses everything from sheet metal to welding to boiler making. The salary of a metal-forming contractor and supervisor has gone up by 32 percent since 2012—and at $65,874, it's not bad. Even normal metalworkers make a not-too-shabby $55,000 a year. The future looks bright, with a projected 1.09 job openings per person in 2020. Metalwork is in high demand and is likely to remain that way for some time.

7. **Pipe-fitting contractor and supervisor.** *Top 50 rank: #23.* By now, you've probably surmised that a job with "contractor and supervisor" in the title is apt to pay pretty well. Pipe fitting is no different: a median salary of $66,560, which has increased 32 percent since 2006. But even journeyman pipe fitters clean up nicely: in Alberta a laborer can make between $40,000 and $50,000. The trade is assembling and maintaining piping systems across a wide variety of venues, from chemical plants to oil pipelines to paper mills. The industry has experienced 46 percent growth in six years.

8. **Electrician.** *Top 50 rank: #31.* When it comes to job growth, electricians knock it out of the park. The industry experienced *100 percent growth* between 2006 and 2012. Median salary is $68,493, no "supervisor" title required. I don't care who you are or where you live: there will always be a need for electricians. Is that a light bulb I see going on above your head?

9. **Mining supervisor.** *Top 50 rank: #43.* Mining supervisor is tied with oil and gas drilling supervisor for the number one spot when it comes to projected job openings, with an expected 2.3 jobs for every person in 2020. People have strong feelings about mining—it's dangerous and highly prone to market ups and downs—but no can argue that the income is good. A mining supervisor makes an average of $64,480 a year managing laborers and coordinating activities, both above ground in quarries and below ground in mines.

10. **Construction inspector.** *Top 50 rank: #48.* At $62,400 a year, construction inspectors make a nice living. These are the guys who inspect buildings to make sure they're safe, structurally sound and up to code, whether it's a 1950s apartment building or a brand new suspension bridge. Most inspectors are hired by the government, which can mean a nice benefit package and cushy pension. If you're a maverick type, you can choose to be self-employed, working with construction and architectural firms in more of a consulting role.

CHAPTER 11

A LETTER TO YOUR 20-SOMETHING, FROM UNCLE KEVIN

Ah, the 20s: that strange wasteland between being a teen-ager and a "real" adult. Today's 20-somethings are firmly grounded in Generation Y, otherwise known as the Millennial Generation. A lot has been said about millennials—they are by and large a confident, open-minded demographic, though numerous studies have documented a marked sense of entitle-ment in the workplace. Gen Yers are said to frequently switch jobs and even careers, always seeking the perfect position that puts their unique talents to use *and* gives them a sense of satis-faction every day.

If you have a 20-something, you know exactly what I'm talking about. And it's that time again: time to hand over this book to your Gen Y kid.

Dear Illustrious Member of Generation Y who believes I should bow down at your feet,

Listen up: you want it all, and I'm sorry to say, you're not always prepared to earn it the hard way, like people of my generation had to. You have high expectations and big dreams. Nothing wrong with that—as long as those dreams and expectations are mixed with a healthy dose of realism and common sense. And I know, the last person you want giving you advice is your folks. Fine. Uncle Kevin's here. You'd better listen to what I have to say.

So you've graduated from university or trade school. Congratulations! The world is your oyster, right? You heard about that one guy in your class who sold his start-up for $2 million a week before graduation—now it's your time to shine. After all, according to you, you deserve a windfall of cash, a closetful of Armani and some really nice dating prospects, right?

Wake up and smell the slow-brewed coffee, my young friend: few waltz into that kind of fortune right out of university. If you're lucky, you will eventually find work that is meaningful and fulfilling, but it's not instant. We've all got to pay our dues.

The 20s are a battlefield. Never before will you have been under so much pressure to spend large amounts of money on things you don't really need—the perfect apartment, the perfect suit. It's like everyone in the world is screaming, "You're finally an adult! Now spend like one!" You've got a legitimate adult job and a nice little paycheck. At first, you're careful. But then you go out for drinks with people from work, and then a couple of nice dinners, and you don't want to look like the cheapskate, so you charge it all to your credit card. Suddenly, you've got a big balance that you can't pay off with your flimsy paycheck, especially while you're bleeding cash on rent for the studio apartment of your dreams. And you really do need a new designer briefcase for work. And look! There's a sale on drapes—wouldn't those look nice in your apartment?

Do you see the problem? All the little expenditures add up—and you may also be paying off your student loans. It's no wonder that most men and women accrue thousands of dollars of debt before their 30th birthday. All this is assuming you can even find a job. Recently, a Statistics Canada report found that of the 1.4 million Canadians who are currently unemployed, almost a third are young people between the ages of 15 and 24. As more young people enter the workforce, there are fewer and fewer jobs available for them. In 2013, the Canadian labor force lost a whopping 39,400 jobs in July 2013 alone. This puts an even greater strain on your finances. If you are unable to find work, you may start leaning too heavily on your credit cards, or worse, crawl back to Mom and Dad and ask if you can move back into your childhood bedroom. And nobody—not you, not me, not your parents— wants that.

Best of luck. You're going to need it.

Uncle Kevin

Money Mistake: *No One Will Hire You*
The Fix: *Embrace the New Reality—Adjust!*

There is some probability that you're not going to get a full-time job the traditional way. And you may not *want* a traditional job— maybe the idea of cubicles and business suits makes your little Generation Y stomach squirm. Or maybe you've been pounding the pavement, trying like hell to get work. Either way, it's time you came to terms with the fact that the world looks different today than it did when your parents were in their 20s. Youth unemployment is currently at a sky-high 19.6 percent, the highest level in 15 years.

What does that mean for you? You're going to have to create your own opportunities. Your 20s are not a time to slack off—far from it. Eleanor Roosevelt and Spider-Man

I worked as a bartender throughout college to help offset my living expenses. I got pretty good at soliciting tips. I also saw the dark side of drinking. There were many nights when I would have to break up fights, help a waitress fend off a drunkard's advances or call an ambulance for a patron who had passed out. I give up drinking for three weeks each January just to prove to myself that I can do it—the weight loss is an added bonus. In this picture I'm embracing my server roots, at a Paris nightclub while out on the town with The Learning Company's European customers.

both agree that with great freedom comes great responsibility. But the inverse is also true: with great responsibility comes great freedom. If you have a skill set, find a way to monetize it. You might end up as a freelancer, hustling for a constant flow of part-time work. Or perhaps you'll find a niche as a consultant. A lot of 20-somethings work as temps—in 2012, 29 percent of Canadians between the ages of 20 and 24 were employed in temporary positions. This can be a great way to work in a variety of companies and wear many different hats, sussing out what you like and what you don't.

Of course, working for yourself puts various stresses on you, too; there are no benefits, no pension plans and little to no job security. You won't know how much money is coming in every month, which can be unnerving at best, terrifying at worse. You probably won't have the opportunity to buy a home—at least not initially—because no one will want to take the credit risk. Buying a house is a huge expense, even if you are married and combine incomes with your spouse. The average household income of a young Canadian couple has climbed 5 percent since 1976, whereas housing prices have climbed 76 *percent*. If you always dreamed of having a house by the time you were 30, it may be time to quit dreaming.

If it looks like you're going to be self-employed for a while, you may want to look into opening an RRSP (registered retirement savings plan) for yourself. The money you put into an RRSP will benefit from tax-deferred compounded growth over the next four decades. The best thing about an RRSP is that you don't have to make big contributions. If you put in $500 a year for the next 40 years, you'll save $77,381. That breaks down to $42 a month, which is the price of a nice dinner out. And you can always up the size of your contribution once you've secured a steady income stream.

There's no scenario where you *don't* want an RRSP. If you're lucky enough to work at a company that offers a matching program, even better. But you should have one either way, because an RRSP is for life. It's a free gift from the government, a way for you to get tax-free returns throughout your working years. RRSPs are basically tax-deferral programs: you invest in them while you're still working. You only pay tax when you withdraw the money from your RRSP the day you retire.

Frankly, putting money into an RRSP is a good idea even if you *do* have a full-time job. Over the last decade, many Canadian companies have closed their traditional defined benefit (DB) pension plans. New employees are often steered into group RRSPs or defined contribution (DC) plans instead. Unlike a traditional DB pension, the DC plans don't pay a guaranteed level of income in retirement. Let's say you're 25 years old when you land a plum position with a $40,000 annual salary and a very competitive DB pension plan. If you work hard for the next 40 years at the same company—assuming steady investment returns and standard compound interest—that pension is going to be worth around $1 million by the time you're 65. But if you start working in the private sector at the same salary, and they only offer you a DC pension plan, you'll be lucky to have *half* a million by the time you retire.

I like to joke that "DC" stands for "debt collector," because that's who is going to be knocking on your door when you're struggling to make ends meet in retirement. So why not start preparing now, while you still have 40 years for that money to accrue interest? Don't leave your future in the hands of a fluctuating job market; start saving now. Sixty-five may sound like the distant future, but it comes sooner than you think.

No matter what, the one thing you absolutely must have is a Catastrophe Cash Fund. This is your Secret 10, and it is *not* the same thing as the money you put into your RRSP. In the event that you take money out of your RRSP, you'll be taxed on it, which worsens your situation. But your Secret 10 is readily accessible in case of emergency. It will come in very handy if you unexpectedly get laid off. Your Catastrophe Cash Fund should be enough to live on for three months at the bare minimum, preferably six. You can whine and moan now, but you'll thank me later. When you fall on hard times, your Catastrophe Cash will keep you fed.

Money Mistake: *You Buy Things to Feel Good*
The Fix: *Feel Good without Buying*

You don't need five pairs of jeans. You don't need 40 blouses. You don't need 25 pairs of shoes. I know a young woman who recently entered the job market who keeps a clothes hamper at work, full of expensive shoes. By my estimates, there's probably $5,000 worth of shoes in there. Talk about a bad use of capital. Nobody needs dozens of designer high heels!

Instead, dress like the French. The French treat their clothes like they treat their wine: they know how to select a few classic items that pair well with anything. Guys can get away with five pairs of shoes. My wife and daughter would kill me if I enforced the same standard on them, so to all the young women out there: seven pairs of shoes. That's all you get. That's me being generous.

Another common money trap is the home makeover. *Do not*—I repeat, *do not*—give in to the siren song of Ikea. The individual items are cheap enough, but by the time you've wound your way through the whole maze of a store, you're apt to have collected $500 worth of disposable furniture. There's no shame in buying things secondhand and accepting hand-me-downs. I have an even better idea: take all that furniture you had in your room at home with you so your parents can have the space back (and breathe a sigh of relief that you're not planning on moving back in as an adult).

Money Mistake: *You Overshare on Social Media*
The Fix: *Protect Your Financial Interests*

A 2012 survey revealed that the average Canadian spends almost an hour and a half a day on social networking sites—Facebook, YouTube, Google+, Pinterest, LinkedIn, Reddit and Twitter, to name a few. But do you know the hidden costs that can come with social media? I'm not just talking about lost productivity (a recent study in the U.K. showed that Twitter and other social networking sites are costing firms approximately £1.38 billion every year). I'm talking about the jobs you're going to lose from prospective employers who don't like what they see on your profile.

CareerBuilder recently conducted an online survey of more than 2,100 hiring managers and resource professionals. They found that 39 percent of companies use social networking sites to get information on job candidates. They didn't always like what they found. When employers stopped considering a candidate for a position because of what they found on social media, these were the most common reasons:

SIX STUPID SOCIAL MEDIA MISTAKES THAT CAN COST YOU THE JOB

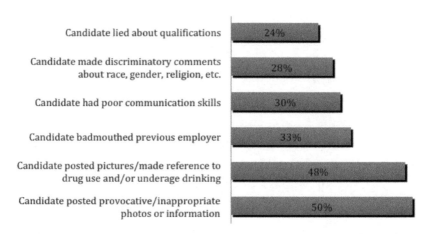

Candidate lied about qualifications	24%
Candidate made discriminatory comments about race, gender, religion, etc.	28%
Candidate had poor communication skills	30%
Candidate badmouthed previous employer	33%
Candidate posted pictures/made reference to drug use and/or underage drinking	48%
Candidate posted provocative/inappropriate photos or information	50%

Source: Chart designed with information from CareerBuilder, Survey by Harris Interactive©, February–March 2013.

If you've got anything online that fits into one of these six categories, you are playing with fire. Racy comments, office gossip, topless photos, pics of you holding a bong—not only are these inappropriate, they're moronic. I've just given you solid proof that employers *do* trawl social networking sites to see what you're like when you're not in your best suit, sitting across the interview table and answering every question with a smile. All it takes is one picture to ruin your future. That one little tag could mean the difference between growing your financial dynasty and remaining unemployed.

Check your privacy settings. Sites like Facebook are constantly changing their platform; even if you think your privacy settings are sewn up tight, they might not be. Keep a close eye on what your friends post. They may think they're being funny, but if they put up photos of you in a compromising position, they are messing with your future. You can ask them to be more circumspect, but ultimately it is your responsibility to monitor your social media presence. Check all your sites at least twice a day, untagging as needed. Last but not least: Google-stalk yourself by setting an alert that tells you whenever your name pops up on the web. What pictures pop up? What personal information? If you find anything even borderline inappropriate, delete it immediately, if possible.

Here's the plus side: use social media well and you look better than other job candidates out there. In the second part of the CareerBuilder survey, 19 percent of the hiring managers said they found something on a social networking site that had caused them to hire a candidate. Topmost among them were candidates who displayed a professional image, about whom the recruiter felt like they got a good feel for his or her personality. Other pluses were candidates who were clearly well rounded, demonstrated great communication skills and had qualifications that matched up with the ones on their résumé.

It isn't just prospective employers who are reviewing what I like to call your "social résumé." When you submit an application for a car loan or a new credit card, those companies are browsing your social media history, too. There are three pillars that go into their decision-making process. The first two have always existed: your track record of employment and your credit score. But the third pillar is a completely new element: the wild, wild world of social media. If you're in alcoholic binge party groups, it's not going to help you get credit.

Your social résumé is a hidden résumé. You'll never know who looks at it. That swimsuit picture or funny one-liner you post is going to be a part of your digital profile *for the rest of your life*. Today's web landscape is unforgiving and unforgetting; spiders scrape everything and keep it. Just because you *think* something is gone from the web does not mean it is gone. Don't let your online past come back to haunt you.

Money Mistake: *You're Going to Grad School to Avoid the Real World*
The Fix: *Follow Dollars, Not Degrees*

By now, we've established that the job market is rough and youth unemployment is at an all-time high. Is it any coincidence that an increasing number of students are opting to pursue graduate degrees? Master's and PhD programs are receiving an epic deluge of applications, and for good reason: nobody wants to face the real world.

If you're considering a career in academia, I urge you to think pragmatically. Ask yourself the following question: What are your chances of getting a job later? A friend of ours has a son who is currently looking at PhD programs in philosophy. He came to the cottage a few months ago, and I asked him how many job openings he thought there would be for professors of philosophy once he completed his dissertation.

"Next to nil," he said. "It's one of the hardest departments to get placement."

I couldn't believe it. This 22-year-old kid was about to spend the next decade of his life reading and writing about dead guys, all so he could get a fancy piece of paper *that would never translate into a paying job*. What was he thinking? Nobody ever gives up a tenured position in a university philosophy department, which means there's no room for the up-and-comers.

There is a big difference between a Doctor of Medicine and a Doctor of Philosophy. Both degrees require a tremendous amount of time and effort, but one invariably leads to some form of employment; the other does not. I'm not saying a PhD in philosophy isn't useful in other ways; I'm just saying there aren't a lot of opportunities to monetize it.

As an author, I work with a lot of talented people in publishing. Few of them have MFAs (Master of Fine Arts degrees). These people are highly successful liberal arts students who've creatively figured out how to monetize their skills. They took an entrepreneurial approach. Instead of going the route of a master's or PhD, they decided to "make their own master's." They took specific courses, enrolled in online classes, handpicked the mentors they wanted to study with at conferences and workshops, and formed their own writing groups (for free). In other words, they amassed experience without amassing debt, and they acquired specific concrete skills that made their résumés unique and showed just how resourceful they were. Did it work? You bet! They're currently working in their dream jobs. Today, they field emails from their penniless writer friends with MFAs begging for freelance work because they can't get hired anywhere!

Here's my philosophy: if you're a creative person, great. Give your creativity an entrepreneurial boost and game the system to your benefit. It's really that simple.

Money Mistake: *You Think You're Too Smart to Be an Intern*
The Fix: *Pay Your Dues*

This may surprise you, but I'm in favor of internships, paid or unpaid. If you can get inside a large organization so they can road test your abilities, great—that *is* a form of payment in the long run. If you apply for an internship and are lucky enough to get hired, work as if you're getting paid $10,000 a week. The interning experience may have immense benefit in the future, whether this company hires you on as a full-time employee or gives you the recommendation you need to land a lucrative position somewhere else.

How do you pay for your life while you're working for free? Go out and get a job. You didn't expect me to endorse going into credit card debt, did you? If you're an unpaid intern, you'll need to make pizza or sling beer at a restaurant. You also need to set a limit on how long you'll work for free. I suggest one year. If you're not offered a permanent job with financial compensation within 12 months, you're probably not going to get one. Time to move on.

Last summer, Savannah was offered two internships with companies she really wanted to work with. Linda and I agreed this was a great opportunity; it was exactly the sort of experience Savannah needed to be competitive in her industry. But she would also need to juggle a job to help pay her way. The three of us sat down together and decided that Savannah would intern during the week and work part time at a vintage clothing store over the weekends. She worked extremely hard that summer at all three jobs. The boost to her résumé has been priceless.

SEVEN TIPS ON INTERNSHIPS

Every summer, we attract a talented group of young men and women to intern at O'Leary Ventures. We run a compliant program, which means we're school-approved. We give our interns a lot of mentorship and real-world experience, and we go to bat for them when they're applying for jobs. They do great work, everything from due diligence to designing the packaging for *Shark Tank* deals.

This year, I sat down with Rebecca Fazio, Ramin Wright and James Laureys to get the "inside scoop" on our internship program. Rebecca is our marketing, branding and design intern. Ramin and James assist with due diligence on deals from *Dragons' Den* and *Shark Tank*.

Here are some great tips from all three interns on how to showcase your talents so you stand out and have a better chance of getting full-time, gainful employment once your internship is over.

1. **Be persistent.** "Hiring interns is never at the top of a company's priority list," says Ramin, "so you need to make yourself stand out. When the president of O'Leary Ventures gave a talk at the University of Toronto, I made sure to introduce myself. After I applied for the internship, I sent him a short reminder email every Monday afternoon to keep my application on his mind." Ramin is right— don't be afraid to be bold.

2. **Showcase your skills.** When we hire interns, we're looking for exceptional young men and women who have set themselves apart. James had extensive experience as a management consultant, working with Fortune 500 companies in consumer goods and retail; during the recruitment process, he also met with angel investors, incubators and venture capitalists. Rebecca's portfolio included

a large range of work in both conventional and unconventional media, and her previous interning experience in design, art direction, PR and social media gave her a unique edge. Ramin ran a profitable media business that sold product-placement spots to national and international brands; he was also studying concurrently for his Juris Doctor and MBA after receiving a dual degree in chemistry and chemical engineering, giving him a broad range of analytical skills. Each of our interns brought diverse talents and backgrounds to the table.

3. **Always have a backup plan.** Rebecca applied for a handful of internships her senior year and considered more than one offer. James met with seven companies in the venture capital industry; he spent two months scheduling meetings and interviews before choosing the internship with us. Ramin applied for nearly 50 summer jobs in addition to applying for the O'Leary Ventures internship. You never want to have all your eggs in one basket.

4. **Go with the flow.** Part of being an intern is learning how to adapt, even if it means doing tasks that weren't part of the original job description. The O'Leary interns are particularly good at this. Ramin says, "On my very first day at the office, I was given the names of 10 companies that I had never heard of and was asked to 'start the due diligence process.' I wasn't sure what any of these companies did or what the 'due diligence' process included! Slowly, I learned what the job entailed and what the boundaries of my purview were. It turned out the real job was 'make Kevin money' and the boundaries were virtually limitless. Being given that kind of responsibility was scary at first, but exciting and motivating, too." Not only did Ramin become a pro at doing due diligence, he was able to put his other skills to excellent use. Turns out he's a Photoshop pro, and when I had a

photo exhibit coming up, he became my technician—and he did an amazing job.

5. **Pay your own way.** To supplement her internship, Rebecca took on freelance design work that she completed in the evenings and on weekends. "I had a part-time job throughout university. I know what it takes to live on a student budget," she says. James supported himself through a combination of savings and loans. "I saved enough to make it through the first year of my MBA and the summer internship," he says. Ramin had saved money from previous jobs and ran a profitable business to boot. He also has an enormous line of student credit. I told him he had better be careful not to rack up enormous debt!

6. **Network, network, network.** All our interns benefit from getting to network with some of the biggest and best in a variety of industries. "I've exchanged business cards with people I never would have come into contact with otherwise," Rebecca says. Ramin now personally knows all 10 celebrity investors on *Shark Tank* and *Dragons' Den*, as well as their teams. "My friends have already begun pitching me new business opportunities!" I took all three interns with me to Los Angeles last week, where they got to visit the *Shark Tank* set and hobnob. "It's been a fascinating experience," James says. "One I'll never forget."

7. **Choose the best, and learn the lessons.** Choose wisely the people you want to intern for, because they could be your mentors and colleagues for a very long time. Over the summer, a major retail chain decided it was not going to sell one of my products. Ramin took the call and listened to a long list of reasons for their decision. When he diligently reported their reasons to me, I picked up the phone and called the retailer back myself. I told them they were out

of their minds. I listed reason after reason why they were making a huge mistake. Guess what? Within five minutes, they reversed their decision. What did Ramin have to say about this? "The biggest lesson I learned during my internship was this: in any business, nothing is set in stone!"

With the family for a relaxing Mother's Day brunch at our local bistro.

PART FOUR

FAMILY

CHAPTER 12

ALL IN THE FAMILY

Tracey Noonan and her daughter, Danielle, sure know how to make an impression. Their product, Wicked Good Cupcakes, first became a media sensation in December of 2011, when a woman had her cupcakes-in-a-jar confiscated by Boston airport security. The transport security officer claimed the unusually "thick layer of icing" posed a risk to national safety. The official response from Wicked Good Cupcakes? "Apparently, we're a tasty terrorist threat."

Fast-forward two years to when I met Tracey and Dani on the set of *Shark Tank*. They were a feisty mother-daughter duo, clearly excited about their product and with the sales to back it up. Dani looked like a young Joan Jett—covered in tattoos, wearing big, dangly earrings, very punk. The Wicked Good origin story went like this: two years earlier, Danielle had moved out of the house, and Tracey suggested they take a cake-decorating class to spend more time together. Together they discovered a mutual love of (and talent for making) cupcakes, and—voilà—a business was born. Tracey's husband, Scott, built the website and handled the tech side of things, so it truly was a family business.

Of course, it won't surprise you to hear I cared more about the numbers than the feel-good family story. When Tracey and Dani made their pitch, they had sold $150,000 worth of cupcakes from January to April—not bad for a little retail shop out of Cohasset, Massachusetts. Their packaging was innovative: they sealed the cupcakes in mason jars to keep them fresh for up to 10 days, then shipped them all over the country. As I pointed out, they didn't have a patent on the jars, so anybody could do what they were doing, but they did have growth potential that the average bakery didn't have. Cupcakes are hot right now, and Dani and Tracey use all the richest ingredients. I know because they brought the Sharks a sample as a part of their pitch. Those cupcakes were obscenely delicious—even if their profits weren't quite as rich as their product. Still, I wanted in.

Tracey and Dani asked for $75,000 for a 20-percent equity in the company. Then Tracey told us the cupcakes cost $2.15 to make and they were selling them to a wholesaler for $3. One by one, the other Sharks bowed out. I hated the margins, but I loved the product. I didn't want equity because I knew I'd never get liquid, so I made them a different kind of deal. "I'll give you $75,000," I said, "if you give me a dollar for every cupcake you sell. After I get my money back, I'll take 50 cents per cupcake in perpetuity."

Things got tense. Mark Cuban told them they couldn't possibly get a worse offer. They left the room to discuss my terms, and Dani got upset. She thought if they did business with me, I would run them into the ground. But Tracey had the opposite reaction. She saw our offer as a loan that would pay sizable dividends. They'd get the money they needed to expand and wouldn't have to give up ownership of the business. Every time they wrote me a check, they were essentially paying for marketing, PR, legal advice and the official endorsement and support of Mr. Wonderful. All in all, not a bad deal—in fact, it was a tasty one.

They countered with 40 cents a cupcake, and in the end we settled on 45 cents in perpetuity.

"Come to Mama," Tracey said when she accepted my offer. We didn't just shake on it, we hugged.

I don't know how or when it started, but my television nickname is "Mr. Wonderful." I knew things had started to get a little crazy when I was met by a driver holding this sign at Los Angeles International Airport.

Wicked Good Cupcakes exploded. Sales skyrocketed to $250,000 the week the episode aired on *Shark Tank*, and again when it re-aired in September. I got my money back in a matter of months. Because I get 45 cents in perpetuity, the checks keep on coming—to me and to them. And because they got the money they needed, Tracey and Dani were able to open up a storefront in Faneuil Hall this summer. That's premium real estate in Boston; every tourist winds up there eventually. Now there are people in

The mother-daughter team of Dani and Tracey Noonan is one of the most successful stories in *Shark Tank* history. They took a commodity like cupcakes, branded them Wicked Good Cupcakes and then came on the show. America loved them and their sales exploded from $15,000 per week to over $200,000! Luckily they are excellent managers, and were able to successfully execute their growth plan. Their business is one of the best investments I've ever made!

New Hampshire who want to franchise Wicked Good Cupcakes because it's enjoying such phenomenal success!

What's their secret? Tracey and Dani aren't afraid to work hard — they were working 13- and 14-hour days when they made their pitch. They're smart and business-savvy, and they're cashing in on one of North America's hottest new trends. But the real story of Wicked Good Cupcakes is the strength of the mother-daughter relationship between Tracey and Dani. When it comes to running a family business, this dynamic duo is doing a wicked good job.

I'm a big believer in entrepreneurship—I wouldn't be on *Shark Tank* and *Dragons' Den* if I wasn't. I'm especially high on businesses where a smart entrepreneur has launched a successful family business. I've seen them in various combos: parent-child, brother-sister, spouse-spouse. It's a beautiful thing when everyone is pulling their own weight, not so beautiful when they aren't. I still remember a young woman from *Dragons' Den* whose family owned a jewelry store. She came onto the show looking for outside investors, but she had five uncles breathing down her neck, watching (and criticizing) her every move. The business was poorly managed because nobody in her family venture had clearly defined roles and everybody wanted to be in control. Remarkably, two Dragons made her an offer, but the company failed to thrive. It filed for bankruptcy barely a year after receiving funding, all because nobody knew how to build a proper team. It was a total disaster.

What about your family? Do you have the kind of strong bonds that would help you succeed in a family business? Your business doesn't have to be giant; it could be an online enterprise or a corner store. Maybe you taught your child how to sew, and now the two of you are thinking about selling pieces on Etsy or eBay. Or your partner has a side business selling antiques and you know you could create a dynamite website because you're a wiz with search engine optimization. If you have a dream of owning a small business, take your dream seriously and run some due diligence on your family unit. Who knows? Maybe your family has what it takes.

Money Mistake: *Your Business Hasn't Made Money After 36 Months*
The Fix: *It's a Hobby, Not a Business—Cut Your Losses and Move On*

Not everyone is cut out to be an entrepreneur. Even those who want to own their own business someday should think long and hard about involving their relatives. The most common mistake I see is when one family member gets really excited and launches something without adequate planning and preparation, pulling the rest of the family down into the vortex. You must be extremely careful and endlessly vigilant. If a business ruins your finances, it's not worth it, because it will probably ruin your family, too.

Set firm benchmarks and stick to them. Wicked Good Cupcakes didn't make money for their first year, and that's okay—most businesses don't. But if your business isn't making money after 36 months, it's not a business; at best, it's a hobby, at worst a money pit. Three years: that's all the time you're allowed to get it right.

Money Mistake: *You Aren't Willing to Make Sacrifices*
The Fix: *Don't Start a Family Business*

Since the opening of their second location at Faneuil Hall, Tracey and Dani have had to make some adjustments. They are still learning how much product to order if they want to fill all their orders with no excess and no shortfall. If they order too many, the cupcakes go to waste and they lose money. If they order too few, they can't fill all their orders and risk making their customers unhappy. "It's like walking a tightrope," Tracey says.

"We're right one week, then the next week we'll order too much."

Like learning anything new, sometimes they make mistakes. "Last week, my husband went in on Sunday to pick up the receipts. When he looked at them, he realized we weren't going to make it to Monday/Tuesday, because we hadn't baked enough cupcakes. It was Sunday, our one day off, but we had to suck it up, go into the shop and bake."

"That's the way it has to be," says Tracey. "Everybody has to be all in." Dani agrees. "Everyone has to be a team player. You can't say, 'It's five o'clock, I did what I needed to do, I'm leaving,' when there's three more hours of baking to do. You've got to give it 110 percent."

Dani has given up a great deal for Wicked Good Cupcakes, too. "I've sacrificed a lot of stuff that other young adults do." Dani doesn't see her friends as much as she'd like because she works a lot, but she is building her very own financial dynasty at an early age, and that's going to pay off big-time in the future. And I helped teach her how.

"We wouldn't be where we are today without Kevin's help. I want him to be proud of Mom and me. I want to keep making him money!"

Danielle is getting married in a few months. The moment I got the invitation, I called her up and insisted she get a prenup. Because of Wicked Good Cupcakes, Dani is a wealthy 20-something, and in my opinion, she's going into this marriage with a lot more at stake than the man she's marrying. I'm sure he's a great guy, but I always advise young people to safeguard their financial dynasties.

***

Elaine Tan Comeau of Easy Daysies Ltd. holds a special place in the *Dragons' Den* hall of fame: she's one of a select few who have incited a bidding war between all five Dragons. Her product was a visual daily routine for kids, a simple magnetic schedule that parents could stick up on the fridge, allowing their children to check off items on their daily "to do" list. Elaine's visual routines were already winning awards by the time she came on the show. She made a great presentation of Easy Daysies, aided by her husband, Ron, and three small children. A self-proclaimed "mom-preneur," Elaine was an investor's dream. Jim Treliving and I went in on a deal together, and though the competition was stiff, we won.

Easy Daysies came from what Elaine calls "the spark of a simple idea." An elementary school teacher, she had been using visual routines with her students in the classroom for eight years. After enough parents asked her to make something for their kids at home, she realized there might be an actual market for her product. She needed $1,400 to make the first batch, so she sold handmade crafts and did extra tutoring until she met her goal. Elaine assembled her first batch of product on her kitchen table between the hours of midnight and 3 A.M., launching Easy Daysies two days after giving birth to her third child. Needless to say, she wasn't getting much sleep!

Before long, Easy Daysies had become the number one Back-to-School Must-Have in *Parents* magazine, and the incoming orders far exceeded the capacity of the Comeaus' kitchen table. Elaine found her way onto *Dragons' Den*, and Jim and I funded the next stage of her business. The rest, as they say, is history.

Money Mistake: *You're in a Rush to Start Your Business*
The Fix: *Do Your Research and Make a Quality Product*

"Google is one of my best friends," says Elaine. "Before I launched Easy Daysies, I logged a ton of time online, making sure there were no other magnetized visual routines on the market. If you have a great idea, the first thing you have to do is make sure it's not already out there. Some people tell me, 'I don't have time for that.' Believe me: the research is the easy part! It gets a lot crazier down the line."

Because Easy Daysies is the only product of its kind, it is filling a massive market niche: Elaine's visual routines are sold in over 600 stores across Canada, and have just launched nationwide at Staples in Canada and Barnes & Noble in the U.S.

This is Linda and me with George in Geneva, Switzerland, where he lives. George is an avid wine collector and is extremely knowledgeable in the Swiss varietals. We sample different styles when we get together, looking for ideas to use in our O'Leary Wines brand.

Elaine has made it a priority to be responsible for what she is putting into the world. "There's a lot of garbage out there," she says. So she makes her magnets out of 70 percent recycled material, and she's recently moved her boxes from 100 percent plastic to 90 percent paper packaging. Don't worry: this hasn't affected profit margins. In fact, it's only garnered the company *more* buzz, landing Easy Daysies a spot on Dr. Toy's Top 10 Socially Responsible Toys of 2012. More buzz translates into more profits, which is good for all of us.

Money Mistake: *You Think a Business Is About Products, Not People*
The Fix: *Don't Neglect Your Relationships*

Elaine Comeau is someone who deeply values her relationships. She's a generous mother and a loving wife, and she brings the same warmth and personal attention to all her business relationships. "I bake for every meeting I go to," she says. "I am trying to build a lasting relationship, not just close a sale. The first retail store in B.C. that sold Easy Daysies still jokes that I am the only supplier who has ever come in with product *and* a fresh-baked batch of chocolate chip cookies!"

While you'll never see me bring fresh-baked cookies to a business meeting, it's a good approach for Elaine. In the industry she's in, it works. But *every* business is based on trust. Any time you can extend a bond and personalize a relationship with a client or supplier, you are adding a tremendous amount of equity in perpetuity. People will want to buy your product or service, simply because they trust you.

Elaine has witnessed the value of adding equity to Easy Daysies through building relationships with her clients. "Something that keeps me going is that I am constantly getting emails from people," she says. "Pregnant moms, mothers of children with autism, parents of foster children. They're all so grateful to have a clear, easy way to organize the day. Easy Daysies has helped these kids stick to their routines and get their homework done on time. And it's not just for kids! I have customers who use Easy Daysies for their parents with Alzheimer's, and I'm working on a teen version, too."

There's no question that people want the product Elaine is selling, so much so that they personally reach out to thank her for the positive impact she has had on their lives. The good news is that Elaine is learning how to develop an expanded product line to service new markets with a much-needed product. That's entrepreneurship at its best.

Money Mistake: *You Think "Family" Means Blood Relations*
The Fix: *Expand Your Definition*

Rob Dyer came onto the *Shark Tank* set wearing his military fatigues. He's an active-duty U.S. Marine Corps aviation officer, and the idea for his product, RuckPack, had first come to him during his second tour with MARSOC (Marine Corps Forces Special Operations Command). "I love the Marine Corps," he says. "I love being active duty, and I love serving my country. But I had bigger plans than to walk around being shot at my whole life."

Rob's "aha" moment came to him in Afghanistan, when he and his fellow Marines were deployed on missions that typically lasted a week or more. The only food they had was what they carried with them. That meant they were virtually all taking some sort of supplement or energy drink, and in Rob's words, "The energy drinks that are out right now suck." As snipers, they needed energy, but the caffeine in products like Red Bull gave them jittery fingers. They needed to recover quickly from dehydration and fatigue, but they also needed to be able to maintain extreme focus and mental acuity. It really was life or death.

At night, Rob and the other Marines would talk about what they wanted to do with their lives after the military; they had become brothers related by a common bond that went beyond blood, and they hoped to find a way to work together outside the military. They knew a lot about supplements, so they started talking about making a product that would provide the acuity and energy they so desperately needed, *without* the unwanted side effects. Those discussions led to RuckPack, a concentrated liquid energy drink of essential vitamins and minerals. RuckPack was the first product brought to market by Noots! Nutrition, the company Rob founded when he returned to the U.S.

When Rob made his *Shark Tank* pitch, it was clear he believed in his product and his company. The Sharks certainly didn't intimidate him. "I'm sure they want me to say building this business was the hardest thing I ever did in my life," he says. "But really, it wasn't." I guess Sharks aren't all that scary compared to the things he'd witnessed in Afghanistan! Rob had no difficulty earning our respect and admiration, as well as our financial backing: Robert Herjavec and I agreed to invest $150,000 in return for 20 percent ownership in the company.

We're glad we did. Since Rob appeared on *Shark Tank* last year, sales of RuckPack have increased 800 percent. Dyer estimates his company is now worth about $1.25 million. Noots! Nutrition is run entirely by veterans and military family members, including a couple of army wives. As CEO, Rob currently employs seven to 10 military colleagues, depending on their deployment schedules.

The fact that the business was born of a Marines mission is no coincidence. "These are men and women I'd trust with my life," Rob says. "And we knew an awful lot about supplements. We all found ourselves thinking, 'Why *shouldn't* we start a company once we got home?' We wanted to invest in our futures. The other choice was to hand our military paychecks over to some fund manager who was a complete stranger. Then I'd have no idea what that money was doing for me *or* my family. That didn't work for me."

Seven military families currently have equity in Noots! Nutrition. They all work together to grow the business, relying on the profits of RuckPack to fund their futures. "Those are my brothers and sisters out there. Some of them are deployed right

It is said that "Old friends are gold." As time passes, I realize how true this is. I made these friends during a period when my balance sheet was upside down and I was technically bankrupt. We all worked at The Learning Company together and the battle to succeed formed relationships that are still strong to this day. Sometimes we celebrate by going away for a weekend. The pursuit of wealth is not about money; it's about freedom. And there is no more noble a cause than that.

now. I owe it to them to keep pushing, because if I can make this business successful, they might be able to come back home sooner. And if I make this as successful as we all want it to be, they might never have to deploy again."

Just as Rob's family dynasty includes his comrades in arms, your "family" could include your colleagues and close friends. What's important is that these are people you can trust and depend on and who bring essential skills to the team. Think of the business world like a war zone, then hire the men and women you are ready to fight alongside every day.

Money Mistake: *Your Product or Service Isn't You*
The Fix: *Monetize Your Unique Skills and Experience*

Rob Dyer is a great example of an entrepreneur who figured out what he was good at and found a way to monetize it. When it came time to develop the product itself, Rob and the other special-ops Marines put their skills to good use. Together they made a list of what they hated about the energy drinks currently on the market, resolving to make a nutritional drink with "no empty energy, no niacin flush, no shakes, no jolt, no crash and no nasty chemical aftertaste." Once they had nailed down a list of the six core functions and identified essential ingredients, Rob started calling manufacturers around the country.

"All the positive things you take out of the military make you a great businessperson or senior staff of a civilian-owned company," he says. Of course, the product isn't just for military; civilians love it, too!

Money Mistake: *You've Surrounded Yourself with "Yes Men"*
The Fix: *Hire Someone Who's Not Afraid to Challenge You*

One of the dangers of a family business is that it can be easy to surround yourself with people who will be too soft. Your mom or husband or baby sis may not want to hurt your feelings, so they won't always tell it like it is. The irony is that the more they cushion you from reality, the more it hurts you. Surrounding yourself with "yes men" or "yes women" is a surefire way to run your business into the ground, because with everyone telling you how great you are, you won't be able to see the problems and fix them in time.

Rob Dyer's wife, Anna, works as the unofficial VP of design. That means she has veto power over all the company's branding and packaging. A while ago, Rob and a handful of other male Marines decided to market an energy drink for women. "We thought we were going to solve all women's problems," Rob says with a chuckle. But when he ran the idea by his wife, she said, "What do you and a bunch of male jarheads know about women?"

It didn't take Rob and the guys long to realize Anna was right. "I was an idiot," Rob said. Lucky for him, his wife was there to keep him in line.

BUILDING YOUR
BUSINESS FAMILY TREE

You can't have a successful business without a great team. But it isn't just who you've got that matters; it's the positions they're placed in. Make sure you pair the right people with the right jobs. Every business is different, but the following five roles are critical for any business, and definitely important in any family venture.

1. **The Bosshole.** Yes, it's exactly what it sounds like. ABC's *20/20* recently did a special on me in which they called me a Bosshole. It didn't hurt my feelings—I took it as a compliment! The Bosshole is the head of the company, though not necessarily the head of the family, and it's not a gender-specific role: women and men can both be Bossholes. The important thing is that the Bosshole can't be sentimental. As a Bosshole, you don't take any crap; you do what you have to do to achieve success for the business. Bossholes never make the mistake of thinking, "It's a family business so I've got to be nice." Be ruthless. Why? Because it's the kindest, smartest move you can make for your family dynasty.

2. **The Positive Partner.** The Positive Partner is the right-hand man (or woman) of the Bosshole. He or she should possess all the traits and skills the Bosshole lacks. This individual is probably the Bosshole's spouse or partner, though he or she may also be another family member with a complementary energy or skill set. The Positive Partner's job is to both support the Bosshole and offer a much-needed balance. You'll know it's a good partnership when the Bosshole has strengths

the Positive Partner is lacking, and the Positive Partner has strengths the Bosshole is lacking.

3. **The No Niece.** If it's the Positive Partner's job to say yes, then it's the No Niece's job to say no. And no, it doesn't necessarily have to be a niece . . . but you get the idea. Think of the No Niece as the opposite of a yes man. It's her job to always be realistic and even cynical, challenging the Bosshole to make sure every business decision is the best one that can be made. If something's not going to work, it is the No Niece's job to point it out, potentially saving the business (and the dynasty) from financial ruin.

4. **The Numbers Nephew.** Again, it doesn't have to be a male and doesn't have to be a nephew, but this individual will be your chief financial officer, even if the title is unofficial. He's fantastic with numbers and he knows everything about the company; he goes to sleep thinking about numbers at night and wakes up thinking about them in the morning. When it comes to crunching figures and keeping your bottom line healthy, his mind works more quickly than everyone else's, which is why you need him around. Whenever you need information, the Numbers Nephew has it at his fingertips.

5. **The Wunderkind.** Think of the most competent manager you've ever seen, and then multiply by five. This is the Wunderkind. She's not an assistant. She doesn't only manage your time, she protects it. She's got her finger on the pulse of the company, which means she's a wiz at human resources. The Wunderkind can juggle 20 different meeting requests and somehow, all due to her fine management skills, you will never miss a single appointment and will always arrive flawlessly prepared for your meetings. She makes sure that deadlines are met, employees are satisfied and clients are happy.

CHAPTER 13

HOPE FOR THE BEST,
PREPARE FOR THE WORST

On my last trip to Switzerland, my stepfather, George, sat me down for a talk. "I've set aside some money for the last years of my life," he said, "and I want every dime of it spent on keeping me in my home until I'm gone." Who could blame him? George has worked hard his whole life, even during his retirement. He retired officially at 60, but even after that he worked as a full-time consultant for the government of the United Arab Emirates, then half time in Russia for the World Bank. He received a steady stream of assignments until, at 74, he finally put his foot down. Now he lives in a beautiful house in Geneva overlooking the lake. If he wants to stay there until they carry him out in a box, he's earned that privilege.

But what if things don't go according to plan? Switzerland has what many argue is the best health-care system in the world, yet even then the costs of long-term care are formidable. What if George is seriously injured or has a stroke? What happens if he needs a home health-care provider to be with him 24/7? Or if he has to be put on life support and hooked up to a bunch of machines? If any of these events were to occur, George would burn through his money fast.

I told him this, which led to a very candid discussion. We talked openly about George's wishes and how tenable they were. It's a hard conversation to have with

Here is my stepfather, George, working on his "to be consulted on my death" document. Preparing his estate this way was a gift to my brother and me. Organizing for the inevitable does not have to be morbid; it was an excuse for us to get together and forced our family to make some decisions while all of us could still participate.

your parents, because no one wants to talk about the finances of dying. But it is a conversation you must have. Many people are finding that their golden years turn out to be not so golden after all. There is nothing wrong with hoping for the best—as long as you prepare for the worst.

The worst can come in many forms. For the aging baby boomer population, it often involves our parents. If there are severe health problems, you may be thrust into the role of caretaker, and your parents could become your dependents—a painful inversion of former roles. The worst could also involve your partner. We all know people who've received that dreaded phone call: "Your husband has been in a car accident." "Your wife has stage III cancer." Some of us may even experience the worst in our own lives: a dire medical diagnosis in the midst of a successful career, health that declines far more rapidly than we imagined.

The bottom line is: life happens. We all hope bad things won't happen to us, but sometimes they do. And I want you to be financially prepared for the worst, even while you hope it never happens.

Money Mistake: *You Think Long-Term Care Insurance Is a Waste of Money*
The Fix: *Get a Quote Today*

Remember those tribal families where parents had to have 12 kids because so few stayed alive? Today is a very different story. A Canadian man born between 1920 and 1922 was expected to live to be 59, a woman to 61. Nearly a hundred years later, those numbers have gone up by 20 years. A baby boy born between 2007 and 2009 in Canada is expected to live to be 79; a baby girl will live a rich, long life of 83 years. By 2020, there will be as many seniors as children. And by 2036, an expected 25 percent of the population will be over 65.

Unfortunately, living a longer life doesn't necessarily mean living a healthier one. As life expectancies climb, the number of seniors who require some form of long-term care continues to rise as well. *Seventy percent of people turning 65 today can expect to use some form of long-term care during their lives.* Put another way, if your parents are in their 60s, their chances of needing long-term care are seven in 10.

"So what?" you say. "We're Canadian—our health care is

covered." Not so fast. Long-term facilities-based care is not publicly insured under the Canada Health Act; it's up to each province to determine precisely which costs are covered and which are not. As a result, costs and services vary widely, and there is little consistency in the level and type of care offered. The government is already struggling under the increasing costs of geriatric medical care. Canada currently spends $3.9 billion a year on Alzheimer's and dementia, and there is no end in sight. By 2031, nearly one million Canadians will be afflicted with dementia.

How much can you expect to spend on a parent or loved one's long-term care? Again, it depends on where you live, but take a look at the chart below:

PRIVATE ANNUAL COSTS OF LONG-TERM CARE FOR NON-MARRIED SENIORS

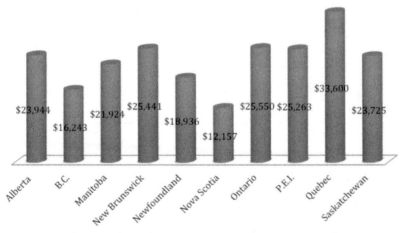

Source: Fernandes, Natasha, and Spencer, Byron G. "The Private Cost of Long-Term Care in Canada: Where You Live Matters." QSEP Research Report No. 443, Research Institute for Quantitative QSEP Studies in Economics and Population, McMaster University of Social Science, October 2010.

These are the average yearly costs, province by province — money that residents and their families paid directly to long-term care facilities, in families where the seniors made an "average" income during their working years ($36,800 before tax in 2008). The numbers are certainly lower than they would be in the U.S., but the rates are not exactly cheap. Private accommodation in long-term care facilities can cost up to $6,000 *per month*. See the table below.

COSTS OF RETIREMENT HOMES/RESIDENCES BY PROVINCE

PROVINCE	PRIVATE ROOM	ONE-BEDROOM SUITE
	COST PER MONTH	
Alberta	$953–4,285	$2,658–4,440
B.C.	$995–3,500	$1,595–5,400
Manitoba	$1,359–2,475	$1,690–3,300
New Brunswick	$800–2,533	$1,943–3,500
Newfoundland	$1,500–1,800	$1,065–4,200
Nova Scotia	$1,705–3,100	$1,900–3,490
Ontario	$1,236–6,000	$1,849–8,000
P.E.I.	$1,825–2,880	$1,950–3,750
Quebec	$850–6,700	$750–2,500
Saskatchewan	$1,380–3,700	$1,200–4,300

Source: LifestageCare ©TakingCare Inc. 2013 (lifestagecare.ca).

When you look at these staggering costs, it becomes clear why I advocate for young people to start thinking early on about purchasing long-term care insurance. Some people say, "But, Kevin, I'm fit and healthy. I don't think I'll ever need it." You don't know that. No one does. According to a recent survey, 74 percent of Canadians admit to not having a financial plan in place should they ever need long-term care. Maybe you're not part of that 74 percent, but your parents are. If so, it doesn't make them bad people. They're simply unprepared, just like the majority of the country.

Hopefully, you are reading this book before tragedy strikes. If so, there may still be time. If your parents are cognizant, open a dialogue. Urge them to invest in a long-term care policy immediately. A good plan will cover them in the event of chronic illness, cognitive impairment (dementia, Alzheimer's), disability and other age-related conditions. Most plans include a waiting period of 30 to 90 days, so the sooner they act, the better. Encourage them to do this *before* they're sick. Premiums can spike sharply depending on a person's health at the time he or she applies.

While you're at it, invest in long-term care insurance for yourself. The younger you start paying into a policy, the better the deal you'll get from the insurance company. A "late starter" might pay premiums up to $5,000 a year, but the costs are lower the younger you are. For example, if you buy in by age 65, the annual premium averages $3,017 for men and $4,838 for women. At 55, you'll be paying in the $2,000 range, and a 45-year-old gets a real bargain: $1,230 for men, $1,912 for women. Those numbers may seem high, but trust me: buying the insurance now is infinitely cheaper than the alternative. When you consider it could cost up to $96,000 for a one-bedroom suite at a facility in Ontario, $1,230 a year is a steal.

Remember: *there is a 70 percent chance you're going to need some form of long-term care.* So stop rolling the dice and make a phone call. Your kids will thank you someday.

Money Mistake: *Your Parents Don't Have a Plan for Retirement*
The Fix: *Help Them Set Aside a Critical 10*

You shouldn't fund your parents' retirement, but there is no reason you can't help them plan for it. In a recent survey conducted by Harris/Decima for CIBC, nearly half of the people polled (44 percent) said they were not financially ready for retirement, and 53 percent confessed to not having a long-term investment plan. With a little time and effort, you can help ensure that your parents have enough money to see them through their golden years without putting a strain on the financial dynasty you and your partner have built.

Grab a pen and paper and sit down with your mom and dad. Draw a line down the page, dividing it into two columns. Write "Income" on the left-hand side and "Expenses" on the right. In the left column, write down every source of income your parents can rely on in retirement. Include all their pension income and any revenue from investments. Also include income from part-time work, rental properties and provision of services. After you write down each item, ask the following question: *Can this number be increased?* That is, do your parents need to restructure their portfolio by increasing the proportion of fixed or guaranteed income, such as bonds or AAA dividend-yielding stocks? This is where a financial advisor can be helpful—someone who knows how to maximize income in retirement.

In the right-hand column, write down your parents' household expenses. Get them to assess as realistically as possible how much money they spend on food, clothing, health care, house maintenance and utilities (including phone and Internet). Keep an eye out for hidden costs they might not think of right away. Do they hire a maid or gardener to help with the house or garden? What about security and alarm systems? How much do they spend on gas, car maintenance and other transportation costs? Most of these expenses can be found in their checkbook or credit card statements. Don't forget to write down costs associated with leisure activities, such as monthly magazine subscriptions, club dues, sporting events, entertainment and any cultural events they attend. Do they travel regularly? Write it all down. After each item, ask the following question: *Can this number be reduced?* Are there certain things your parents can do less frequently, or make do without? The goal is to patch up any existing money leaks, creating a reserve for long-term care and other unexpected events.

I talked about setting aside a Secret 10 early in life; now is the time for a Critical 10. This money is to be used in case of emergency. The Critical 10 should amount to roughly 10 percent of expenses. If your parents' expenses amount to $4,000 a month, they need to be setting aside $400 each month for their Critical 10.

If possible, take your parents to meet with your financial advisor. He or she will be able to help them look at their options, possibly moving their money into more appropriate investment vehicles. If there's still a deficit every month—and if your parents are still healthy and active—they might consider continuing to

231

work part time in retirement. Many seniors don't want to stop working; they enjoy having something to do. If your parents have a technical skill or a professional background, perhaps they will want to make themselves available for part-time or consulting work the way my father did. As he says, "It gave me the satisfaction of knowing I was still useful to society, even though I was old and gray."

Money Mistake: *You're the Primary Caretaker for Your Parents*
The Fix: *Pay Yourself a Salary—You Deserve It*

Many Canadians today find themselves in the difficult position of being the primary caregiver for their ailing parents. If this describes you, you need to protect yourself and your family. First, go to your siblings and see if they are willing to donate time or resources. They may be able to help out so that the burden does not fall entirely on your shoulders. If you are an only child, however, or your siblings are unavailable (or unwilling) to assist you, I suggest you talk to your parents. Explain to them the costs of caretaking. You may have to quit your job or work shorter hours, which will necessarily affect your compensation. Make a financial arrangement with your parents to ensure that you are paid for your time.

If that makes you uncomfortable, get over it. Your parents are the last people in the world who would want to put you in a situation where you are working for no pay. If your parents are senile, just know that if they still had their wits about them, they would want you to put yourself and your own family first. That's what they did with you, right?

Your parents may elect to compensate you for your time by giving you a bigger chunk of their inheritance once they pass. You'll want to discuss that with them, too. Make sure everything is in writing, indisputably recorded in their will. Maybe you've got three brothers who haven't lifted a finger while you've been breaking your back as a full-time caretaker. You've given your parents a tremendous gift. Do you deserve more money than your brothers? Sure you do. But the cold hard truth is that if your gift of time, love and resources is not reflected in your parents' will, there is nothing you can do about it.

Julia, who is a friend of Linda's and mine, is a high-powered professional whose mother is in a long-term care facility and needs someone to offer one-on-one care several times a week. Because Julia's brother lives five minutes away from the facility, he is providing a lot of that care. The agreement that Julia and her brother have is that when their mother passes, he will get proportionately more of the inheritance. It's in the will. Julia is relieved and grateful to her brother and understands he should be compensated for all his work. In her mind, it isn't just a gift he is giving to her mother; it is a gift to Julia, too.

A quick note: an inheritance is a gift passed from your parents' lives to yours, and there is only one honorable way to use it. *That money has to reduce debt.* The minute you get it, keep 10 percent for your Secret 10 and use the rest to pay off the mortgage and any medical or credit card debt you have accrued. *Do not let yourself spend it on anything else if you have debt.* Pay off your debt first. Then and only then can you pass any extra on to your kids—and only if you want to.

Money Mistake: *You Lost Your Job, but Haven't Changed Your Lifestyle*
The Fix: *Go Back to Your 90-Day Number and Cut a Third of Expenses*

At a recent book signing, a man came up to me who had worked in the same industry for the past 28 years. He was making $200,000 a year when he got laid off. The guy was 55 years old and no one would hire him. "I don't know what to do, Kevin," he said. "I'm supposed to take my whole family to Hawaii next month. We've been planning the trip for years. I can't cancel it."

I told him he not only *could* cancel it, he *had to*. Then I instructed him to go back to the 90-Day Number worksheet in my book. "Then cut one-third of your expenses until you can find another job," I suggested.

Families get in a lot of trouble when Mom or Dad loses a job. What usually happens is that they don't adjust their lifestyles. They're living under the assumption that Mom or Dad will get another job soon. But in today's economy, most people don't get rehired immediately; it could take months or even years.

If you or your spouse loses a job, you must *immediately* go back to your 90-Day Number. Redo the worksheet in chapter 6, this time cutting one-third of your expenses. Involve your kids in the discussion. Do it as a family, because you will all need to make adjustments in the way you live. Betty's not going to summer camp. You won't be buying a car and you won't be going on vacation. Drop your magazine subscriptions and cut your fitness center membership. You'll be running on the open road.

Money Mistake: *You Got a New Job! Time to Spend!*
The Fix: *Learn the Lesson: Savings First*

Four months after getting laid off, Mom gets a new job at the same level. The family starts spending like crazy. "Great!" they say. "We can get back to our old lifestyle."

Not so fast. It's time to get the whole family around the dinner table once again. You should be using *all* of Mom's new income to reduce debt and to save in case this happens again one day.

The good news is you understand that jobs are tenuous, and no matter how good you are at what you do, you could lose a whole career in a split second. So you'll make adequate preparations this time, shoring up your family dynasty. You'll pay off your debt and start saving everything you can in your Secret 10 in case a layoff strikes again in the future.

Money Mistake: *Thinking About the Expense of Death Feels Wrong*
The Fix: *Face the Funeral Music*

Death is sad. No news there. It's not great for our finances, either, bringing with it unexpected costs and hidden fees. Everybody is going to deal with death—and there's a whole industry that profits from it.

A traditional burial can start at around $5,000, but with all the extras, you could easily end up spending $15,000—the great irony being, of course, that the person you are spending that money on won't be there to appreciate it.

Funeral directors make their livings off of the bereaved. Remember: they're salespeople. Beware of phrases like "I know you want what's best for your father," and "This is the last thing you can do to honor your mother." You want another piece of advice? Don't do an open casket. You pay a premium for them, but they don't honor your loved one's death or life.

Now let's talk about the casket itself. Here's a little-known secret: you can buy caskets online from Walmart or Costco that are just as nice as the ones in the showroom and cost thousands less. Those who are environmentally conscious can even choose a rental casket, a thick cardboard container that is removed before burial or cremation. If there are no low-cost caskets in the display room of the funeral home, ask to see one anyway. Believe it or not, some places hide them in the basement—out of sight, out of mind.

Deciding between cremation and burial can be a difficult and painful decision. Only you know what's right for your family; all I can do is provide some financial facts. As a general rule, the cost of cremation is one-quarter that of a burial. Simple cremations start around $600, though if you get all the extras—the obituary notice, the viewing—it can cost up to $4,500. Cremation costs vary by province; a low-cost cremation can be obtained for $587 in Quebec, $995 in Vancouver and $1,400 in Toronto. In certain provinces, the cost is higher—in New Brunswick, for example, a simple cremation can cost close to $3,000. It's considered morbid to discuss a funeral, let alone plan for one. *But you must have these conversations now.* Open the discussion with your parents and with your partner.

Also, decide on a course of action if one of you were to have a serious accident or contract a debilitating illness. Discuss your feelings about a DNR (do not resuscitate) order. If we are honest with ourselves, most of us would never want a loved one to keep us hooked up to a machine if we were brain-dead, draining our loved one emotionally and financially. But if you don't let your feelings be known now, you're not preparing for the worst. And that is the cold hard truth.

FOUR QUESTIONS YOU NEED
ANSWERED *BEFORE* THE END

You've heard the saying: nothing is certain except death and taxes.
(Don't even get me started on the death tax.) Give the following list
to your parents and discuss their answer to each question. Go over it
with your partner, too.

1. **Do you have a will?** I don't care if you're only 30 years old: if you have
    kids, you need a last will and testament. Choose a lawyer you trust,
    someone who will write crystal-clear clauses that leave no room for
    misinterpretation. Your feelings about your prospective beneficiaries
    may change over time, but don't use that as an excuse to put it off
    indefinitely. You can always change your will—most people do at
    some point. Budget around $300–$400 for a lawyer to draw up a
    will (add an additional $100 for a power of attorney). If you want a
    more cost-effective option, you can download a legal will on sites like
    FormalWill.ca for under a hundred bucks. If you don't have significant
    assets, tax concerns and multiple beneficiaries, this is often a great
    option. It covers all the basics, including whom you want to act as
    legal guardians of your children in the event of your death.

2. **Have you created a file for your surviving family members?** My
    father, George, has an actual file folder in his house with a label that
    says: TO BE CONSULTED ON MY DEATH. Both my brother, Shane,
    and I know exactly where it is. On the sad day that George passes
    away, at least we won't be scrambling. The file should include all the
    steps to take before your will is probated, including tax assessments
    and a potential phone call to the bank. (If you have money in a joint

account with your partner, you may need to notify the bank to make sure the account holder's names are separate so that your money isn't frozen in the event that one of you dies.)

Indicate where important documents can be found, such as property deeds, tax papers, insurance and medical claims. You'll probably want to keep your birth certificate, passport, social insurance number and any other official, hard-to-replace documents in a separate place for safekeeping. Safe, lockbox or safety deposit box at your bank—the choice is up to you. Just be sure to include the code or security combination in your "to be consulted on my death" file. To be extra safe, scan each of these documents so you have digital copies as well.

Write down a list of the people or entities to be notified of your death. I don't mean friends and distant relatives—though you should write those down, too—but the people who will need an official copy of the death certificate. These include: the civil authorities in your province, your financial advisor, the lawyer who drew up your will, your pension fund providers, your health insurance, other insurance companies, your various credit card providers, the office that issued your driver's license and your tax accountant (if someone else handles your taxes). List email, phone and any other available contact info for each of these people. Again, you're trying to make it as easy as possible for your grieving family members.

If you own real estate, indicate the address and expected resale value of each property. This can help your beneficiaries decide whether to keep, sell or rent the property in question.

3. **Have you made funeral arrangements?** You can plan out every detail of your funeral, right down to the musical accompaniment and how many cocktail onions will be served in the drinks.

I've made my pitch for cremation, but there's no shame in a traditional burial. When I graduated from university, one of the girls in my class took a sales job at a well-known cemetery. She needed sales badly, so I started buying plots from her. Over the years, I amassed eight plots and eventually consolidated them into one location. My mother is buried there, and there's space for my entire family when we pass on. Today, those plots have gone up in value so much that they are one of the best investments I've ever made!

4. **Have you written down all of your email and social media passwords?** I can't stress how important this is. Write down the login ID, password and PIN number for every single site you use (and your computer itself). Bank websites, sites for auto and property insurance, Facebook, Twitter, and any and all email accounts. You probably have login information stored at more websites than you think, so be thorough. If you don't do this, your partner or grown child could spend many hours on the phone, trying to cut through the bureaucratic red tape. Time is money: don't waste theirs.

CHAPTER 14

MIDLIFE CRISES & MONEY MISMANAGEMENT

Every summer, my wife and I attend a dock party across the lake from our cottage in Muskoka. It's been a regular event for decades. When it started 20 years ago, everybody attending was married. There must have been at least 50 couples, and we all brought our kids. Trevor and Savannah have been going to that party since they were two years old.

But a few years ago, Linda and I began to notice a change. Half the couples were divorced. The men still came to the dock party, but instead of bringing their kids, they brought their new, much younger girlfriends. These guys were spiraling headfirst into midlife crises and they were competing with each other to see who had the most attractive young girl on his arm. The dock party was no longer a celebration of the family dynasty; it was a testament to a lot of broken homes.

Last fall, we were having dinner with some friends in Muskoka when the conversation found its way to the dock party. Our friend Denise, longtime wife of Larry, had had enough of this insanity.

"That's *it*," she declared. "I've been going to this party for the last two decades, but no more. I am 52 years old. I've had three kids. I am not going to sit around a dock with a bunch of 20-year-old bimbos primping and pouting in their bikinis. Larry and I will not be attending unless all those girls are gone."

Everyone went silent. Then Linda leaned over and whispered to me, "It's about time."

This declaration became known among our friends as the Denise Decree. The Denise Decree resonated through our group like a lightning bolt. And Denise was such a respected and well-liked matriarch that her decree was actually adopted as a rule for the dock party: no young bimbo girlfriends allowed.

One longtime male attendee who'd divorced one of Denise's friends actually asked her for special permission—"Can't I get grandfathered in? I've been with my 28-year-old girlfriend for three years!" The answer was no. The Denise Decree was law. No exceptions.

Both Linda and I supported Denise 100 percent. Here was a woman who had worked tirelessly to create a family dynasty. She had made endless sacrifices, raising three great kids while Larry was off working to build the family fortune. She'd supported many business pursuits, and she'd always gone the extra mile to make the dock party great, even though she wasn't the hostess. Denise was a role model for all of us, and especially for all the women her age who'd protected, raised and managed stable families for decades.

I talk at length about gold diggers in my second book, but suffice to say that most of those young ladies are after one thing and one thing only: a middle-aged man's wallet. I know one story of a young gold digger who regularly costs her middle-aged man $50,000 per weekend in shopping trips. Not only is that financial suicide, it's also cheating his wife and family of what should be their legacy, their dynasty.

Ladies: if your man is going through a midlife crisis that affects not only your relationship but your bank book, make sure you protect yourself. The Denise Decree should be your inspiration. Either your husband reconfirms his stake in your relationship and in building the dynasty, or he's out. And if leaving is the only option, fine—as long as he hands you your rightful half of the family fortune.

Money Mistake: *A Midlife Crisis Threatens*
The Fix: *Save the Dynasty at All Costs*

Ah, the midlife crisis—the Achilles' heel for men of a certain age. We've all seen it happen. Half my friends are divorced, some of them multiple times. After watching these guys enter into second, third and even fourth marriages, I've come to realize that their partners are not the problem; it's *them*. What they fail to realize is that the bling-bling of youth and beauty vanishes faster than a mirage in the desert. The payoff is in the dynasty, not the 20-year-old girlfriend. But so many guys lose their heads—and then they lose their wallets, too.

Take my friend, for instance. We'll call him Mark. Mark is something of a legend in Boston: he's had four partners (though technically only three wives) and *six children*. I don't even advocate having six kids with *one* partner, let alone four! The guy is embroiled in lawsuits every day! His ex-wives all know each other—they call themselves the Ex-Mark's Club—and every one of them is intent on clawing a piece of Mark's financial dynasty. Oh, and these women aren't gold diggers; they're moms. You can't blame them for wanting to secure a future for their children, even if their future with Mark didn't pan out.

Mark is only 45 years old. He should be stabilizing his empire, not dividing it into pieces. But every time he gets divorced, he suffers from a geometric decrease in wealth, because each wife takes her deserved half. All the Ex-Marks are suing for child support, too, and rightly so. This makes Mark's life incredibly complicated.

Mark is a charming guy, so I can see why women fall for him. He's a wealthy entrepreneur, offering each new partner the illusion of ease and security. The irony is that they really do get a lifetime of ease and security, at least financially, even after Mark has moved on, because he's forced to leave half of everything behind.

The costs of Mark's choices are tremendous. But there's only one person responsible, and that's Mark! He keeps chasing the dream of happiness and fulfillment in the shape of a short skirt. It's hell on his bank account and confusing for his kids. Linda and I are pretty good friends with his third ex-wife, and she says it's been heartbreaking for their young son, too. Mark Jr. can't keep up with who's who. He gets ferried from his mom's house and then to his dad's, and at his dad's he can't keep track of the changing women. You know who's going to be paying that kid's therapy bills in a few years? Mark, that's who.

Mark's oldest kids are in their 20s. They're resentful, and they're quickly racking up more expenses for Daddy. To complicate matters, Mark's latest girlfriend had a baby a few weeks ago. Any hopes

Mark had of putting some pieces of his first family back together just flew out the window. His midlife crisis cost him his dynasty.

I'm not claiming any moral superiority over anyone, and I'll be the first to say that if you think marriage is a walk in the park all the time, you're kidding yourself. All relationships have their ups and downs, their own trials and tribulations. Linda and I have had our share of struggles. But I'm happy to say our marriage has survived through it all, and today it's stronger than ever before. Hold firm, remember your values — and your net worth as a couple — and all will be well.

Money Mistake: *Your Partner's Bad Habits Are Becoming a Financial Burden*
The Fix: *Issue an Ultimatum Before All Your Investments Are Drained*

Most men (and women) get over their midlife crises. The smart ones realize that what they have in a marriage — or in any long-term relationship — is valuable. They're never going to have that depth of history with a new partner, no matter how perfect, sexy or desirable that partner may seem. A wise man will choose the dynasty over the arm candy, the true wealth over the short-term bling.

But some midlife crises manifest themselves in other ways. It's not always the hot young thing that causes a breach in the family dynasty; it could be addiction or other reckless behaviors. Your partner still feels that something is missing, so he or she tries to fill the void in other ways. Alcohol, drugs, gambling and excessive debt all pose a serious threat to your investments. And I'm not just talking about your stock portfolio: I mean the investments you've made in your partnership and in your family dynasty. While divorce is costly, there are times when it may actually be *less* costly than remaining together.

I recommend a three-strikes-you're-out policy. If your partner struggles with any of the following, give him or her three chances to get help. But if your partner slips back into old habits after the third time, it's a deal breaker. Get out while you can.

Alcohol/Drugs

According to a study by the Canadian Centre on Substance Abuse, alcohol abuse costs the nation a whopping $14.6 billion each year. That includes $7.1 billion in lost productivity due to illness and premature death, $3.3 billion for direct health-care costs, and $3.1 billion for enforcement costs. Break that number down and every Canadian citizen is paying $465 a year to fund the country's alcoholics.

My birth father, Terry, was a borderline alcoholic, so I've seen firsthand how alcoholism can wreak devastation on

Me with my father, Terence O'Leary, in 1958. Although he died just a few years later, I still have memories of him. He was a classic Irishman: very gregarious with many friends. He was a fantastic salesman, something I'm proud to say I inherited. I was not surprised when Peter Munk, the founder of Barrick Gold, called me one day out of the blue to tell me that he had traveled with my father from Ireland to North America in the late '40s. He had only good things to say about my dad.

a family. If after three stints in AA, therapy or rehab, your partner is still unable to stay away from the bottle, your marriage is in trouble and you should walk away.

I'm not saying you and your partner can't drink. One of my businesses is O'Leary Fine Wines, which Linda and I co-own. We both love a nice glass of wine, and creating our own label has given us a lot of joy. But I've always known alcoholism was in my genes, so I have been very careful about drinking in moderation, modeling the same thing to my kids. Linda and I have tried to foster a healthy relationship with alcohol. I want my children to understand that leaning too hard on alcohol will bleed them dry, drop by drop, penny by penny.

I'm less lenient on drug use. You never know who's going to become the addict; it could be you or it could be somebody else. Bottom line: drugs destabilize the family dynasty. They have a negative impact on your net wealth (illegal drugs cost Canada $8.2 billion a year). Any family that has major problems with alcohol or drugs is going to suffer.

Gambling

According to a 2011 Statistics Canada report, more than 70 percent of Canadians with an after-tax income of $40,000 or more partici-pate in at least one gambling activity. Most common are govern ment lotteries, with other lotteries and raffles in second place, followed by casinos, slot machines, video lottery terminals and bingos. Fortunately, the average annual household expenditure on gambling tends to be under $500, which means the majority of Canadians are keeping themselves in check. But if your partner has an addiction to gambling, you'll know it—because, apart from the severe emotional toll, your finances are going to take a massive hit. Again, I advise giving your partner three chances to curb his or her behavior and seek help. But after that, you've got to get away.

Debt

Bad money choices of all other kinds—even when not related to addictions—are pernicious and destructive. No matter how much you love your partner, if he or she is sinking deeper and deeper into debt, it's time to call it quits. You must protect your family dynasty, even if it pits you against your partner. Unfortunately, if you've tried three times and haven't succeeded in eliciting lasting change, you've got no other choice.

Here's something interesting: on my list of deal breakers, you may notice that infidelity didn't make the list. That's because it is easier to address than financial problems. Don't get me wrong: it is still indescribably difficult to reestablish trust after an affair. But unless the infidelity is indicative of a more deeply ingrained addictive behavior, it is often something a couple can work through.

If you or your partner has cheated, it's time to ask some hard questions. First: Why'd you do it? Second: Can you fix it? Hopefully, the answer to that second question is yes. Your goal is to avoid a divorce at all costs, because the minute you involve a lawyer, you'll start to bleed assets, not to mention rip your family apart. Bring in a therapist or a mediator if that's what it takes. This can be costly, but it's still a lot cheaper than divorce. Ladies, here's your chance to enact your personalized Denise Decree. Gentlemen, here's your chance not to screw it up.

A DECADE-BY-DECADE GUIDE TO
MANAGING YOUR ASSETS

Below, you will find a decade-by-decade guide to managing your assets. If you follow the advice here, you'll earn yourself some financial peace and security later on and you'll also ensure that your family dynasty stays safe, even in the moments when you're tempted to throw it all away.

THE 30s

During your thirties, you should be entirely focused on *paying off debt*. Work like mad, even if it means making sacrifices, like not buying the boat you've been salivating over or not going on that fancy vacation. If you're like most people, you're still paying off your student loans in your 30s, so do that and don't make the mistake of getting a new debt to replace your old one. After the 30s, no more debt. That's your goal.

THE 40s

If you haven't paid off all your creditors, it's time to get serious. The year I turned 40, I decided I had to pay off everything, fast. Between the ages 35 and 42, I worked insane hours seven days a week toward that goal. By 42, I had no mortgage and no credit card debt. I had no debt at all. All I had was savings. And I kept saving throughout my 40s so that I could treat myself to a little luxury in a few years . . . but I had to earn it first.

THE 50s

If you did what you were supposed to in your 30s and 40s, you've won yourself a little breathing room. By now, you've paid down your debt and saved up a lot of money; your career is going well. You can afford to reward yourself. For me, that reward took the shape of a Porsche; consider what's appropriate for you. Channel all your midlife angst into this luxury purchase. Just remember: *you cannot splurge unless you have a really good nest egg.* If you've got one, great. Get yourself a little gift. You deserve it.

THE 60s

In your 60s, you are rehearsing for retirement. You should know your 90-Day Number inside out and know how to strike a balance between what you invest and what you spend. Live within your means, and do not deplete your principal. You don't know how long you're going to live, so spend like you'll live to be 100. By now, you should be a fine-tuned financial machine.

CHAPTER 15

GIVE YOUR MARRIAGE A FIGHTING CHANCE— AND IF THAT DOESN'T WORK . . .

Emotions are expensive. Whether you're madly in love or spitting mad, your wallet will take a hit. Think about it: at the beginning of a relationship, so many people ply their lovers with champagne and caviar. At the end of it, they're coughing up $400 an hour for a good divorce lawyer. It seems the more intense the emotions, the higher the cost.

If you are contemplating divorce, this chapter is for you. I'm going to work very hard to help you separate the emotional aspect of divorce from the financial aspect. A divorce will savage your savings and decimate your dynasty. Thank goodness you're reading this book, because I am about to save you from one of the biggest mistakes you could ever make.

Money Mistake: *A Divorce Isn't That Expensive, Right?*
The Fix: *Consider the Unexpected Costs*

In my last book, I reviewed the up-front costs of divorce—uncontested versus contested, plus the extra costs of a separation agreement and/or child support agreement. Here's the thing: the legal fees themselves don't seem so bad. Sure, you'll probably spend a few thousand on attorneys' fees and court costs, but anything's better than living with the ol' battle-ax, right?

Wrong. Of the 70,000 divorces in Canada each year, the majority of cases end up snarled in legal snafus, dragged out by arbitrary motions and affidavits. A study by the Law Society of Upper Canada found that when children are involved, it takes an average of three years for a litigated divorce in Ontario to blunder through family court. That's three years of near-constant attorney fees.

If you or your partner own real estate, you can tack on a whole new layer of expenses. There are refinancing costs, record deed fees, and of course there's that pesky attorney again, billing you $400 an hour to iron out all the kinks.

If you have kids, they are going to be living between two homes. That may not seem like a big deal, but they're going to need more stuff. Now they have two wardrobes, two closets full of clothes—maybe even two computers. And how about all the discounts you got as a couple on the expenses you shared? Car insurance, cell phones, cable, Internet—you're paying for all of that on your own now. Separated couples often report that their expenses increase by $20,000 to $30,000 a year.

Money Mistake: *You Want a Divorce*
The Fix: *Give Yourself a 90-Day Cool-Down*

So you caught your partner with someone else. Or maybe you're the one who feels the need to call it quits on your marriage and pursue other options. Whatever happened, once there's a confrontation between you and your partner, tempers are hot and your partnership is sinking faster than a camel in quicksand. One of you speaks the dreaded words "I want a divorce." What happens next?

Don't do anything for 90 days. Remember, right now you are a slave to your emotions, and emotions cost money. I want both of you to take a 90-Day Cool-Down. If you can't bear the sight of your spouse, stay with a friend or relative. Check into a hotel if you must, though it's best if you can avoid spending any money. No lawyers, no ultimatums, no threats. Just wait. It's only three months.

Of course, it can be hard to think rationally during the 90-Day Cool-Down, to protect the family dynasty you've built. After three months have passed, reconvene and see where you both stand. If there's a way to salvage your marriage, do it. If not, I maintain that you are both in a far more relaxed place to open a dialogue now than you were three months ago, and you are less likely to make rash and costly mistakes.

Money Mistake: *Your Relationship Is Dead*
The Fix: *Get a Shadow Divorce Instead of a Paper One*

If you decide the best thing to do is end the partnership, that's okay. But that doesn't mean you absolutely have to dissolve the dynasty. Most people assume their ex wants to "screw" them by hiding assets during the divorce process. Each side lawyers up, arming themselves for battle, and the Great Cash Waste begins. You might as well give $100 bills to everyone around the conference table, pass around a Zippo and tell them to light them on fire. Divorce lawyers are just programmed to take advantage of your emotional distress.

There's another option, especially for those over 60. If you both admit the partnership is over, map out a plan to monetize and split your assets without going through a costly paper divorce. That's a "shadow divorce." It's simple: if you own a home, sell it. If there's a mortgage, pay off the remaining debt and simply divide the cash 50/50. Each party should set up their own account in their own name. Furniture or other non-liquid assets can be divided between the parties or sold.

The one caveat here is that if you sell your house, you'll have to pay taxes on capital gains. This can be financially devastating, especially if your home has been in the family a long time, because approximately a third of the value will be going to the government.

If you own other real estate besides the family home, consider not selling it; this way, you avoid bleeding out your assets in capital gains tax. Let's say you and your partner own a modest cottage that you bought for $100,000 30 years ago; it's worth $1 million today. You and your spouse are not going to reconcile. In a shadow divorce scenario, it's better for you to figure out a way to keep the cottage and split the time you use it amicably than sell it. It's simple math: you've got a $900,000 capital gain on the cottage. The TCG, or taxable capital gain, is half of that, so $450,000. If you're in the highest marginal tax bracket, you'll owe 45 percent to the government. That means when you sell the cottage, you're going to owe $202,500 in capital gains tax. Split that down the middle and you've each given up $100,000! That's insane and unnecessary. Why not agree to the cottage remaining a joint asset? Each person gets to use it for six months a year. If you can agree to that, you're going to save $200,000. Remember how I told you that every asset should be owned jointly? This illustrates why.

In the right context, a shadow divorce can be highly effective. (It works best when all children are grown and out of the house.) By sidestepping a real divorce, you won't have to get the government involved or pay thousands of costly attorney fees. But you will need to hire a lawyer to draft a letter crystallizing your separation date. That little date is a big deal: it's the date all your family assets stop accumulating. If you or your spouse loses or makes money after that, it's not pertinent; your joint assets are locked in at the monetary value that they had on your separation date. So get that letter and then don't call your lawyer again—you won't have to. You can still receive the tax benefits of marriage without the emotional stress of staying with someone you no longer want to share your life with. The beauty of this strategy is that the legal option of divorce is always open if, for some reason, you want to go through that later. In the meantime, you have saved tens of thousands and can get on with your life—in a better financial situation.

Money Mistake: *Your Kids Are Following in Your Footsteps*
The Fix: *Set Them Up for Success*

Did you know that children of divorce are far more likely to get a divorce themselves? Daughters of divorced parents have a

60 percent higher divorce rate than daughters whose parents stayed together, and sons have a 35 percent higher divorce rate. Those are seriously sad statistics.

You can't micromanage your child's love life, but you *can* put structures in place to preemptively protect their financial dynasties. James Laureys, the intern we met in chapter 11, is a recipient of this kind of protection. His mother went through a long and costly divorce. Determined to save her son from the same fate, she put a condition in her will that in order for James to receive any inheritance, he had to sign a prenuptial agreement with his partner before getting married. It took the pressure off her son to have a difficult conversation, and he could explain to his prospective wife that this wasn't *his* idea, but his mom's final wish! How could she argue with that?

What a fantastic gift from a brilliant financial strategist. James's mother learned from experience, and in so doing, she saved her son a ton of financial and emotional heartbreak down the line. What a beautiful way to pass along a financial legacy and to ensure that it gets into the right hands.

DEBUNKING FOUR
END-OF-MARRIAGE MYTHS

In my circles, I meet a lot of smart and interesting people. Yet I am always surprised by how many intelligent men and women cling to certain myths. In no area are these myths more prevalent than on the topics of divorce and separation. Getting a divorce is hard enough without having to sort through lies and misinformation. Here are the three most common myths I hear—and the actual truths behind them.

MYTH #1: It is illegal to remain married to your spouse after you've agreed to a shadow divorce.

If you no longer want to live with your spouse, you don't have to; there's no rule saying you can't separate. A shadow divorce is simply a way of reconfiguring your living arrangement so that you retain all the benefits of being married while living under separate roofs and maintaining separate accounts. You'll also avoid the exorbitant legal fees of getting a divorce. The only time it can get sticky legally is if you don't have the house in both of your names. Luckily, that won't matter, since you've put all your assets under joint ownership, right? (If not, reread chapter 5.)

MYTH #2: Ending your common-law relationship is much easier than getting a divorce.

In the most basic sense, this is true. To end a common-law relationship, you simply have to end it, no divorce papers required. But when common-law couples have children and/or assets—as most do—they often find themselves resorting to legal action when it comes to child custody or the division of property.

When a married couple divorces, the general rule is that if the value of assets increased during the union, that increased value is shared equally. *This is not true for common-law relationships.* Let's say the house you've lived in with your common-law partner for the last 15 years was not purchased in a joint ownership—it is only under your partner's name. You're going to have to prove that you are entitled to a share of that house. You'll either need to show that you made a financial contribution toward the purchase, or you will have to demonstrate to the court your contributions of time and effort (raising the kids, managing the household, etc.). If you can't prove this successfully to the court, your spouse could walk away with everything.

The easiest way to protect yourself from financial ruin is to simply sign a cohabitation agreement with your common-law partner. I covered these in detail in my last book, but here's a quick recap: this is a written agreement that lays out how you will deal with your property should your relationship end. You should absolutely include a clause in your cohabitation agreement that makes you and your partner subject to the same family law rules governing division of property for married couples.

MYTH #3: Going on a spending binge in the twilight of your marriage feels great, and you're spending your soon-to-be ex's money, not your own!

Wrong. It *does* cost you. If you "treat" yourself to a decadent shopping spree, splurging on a new home-entertainment system or 12 pairs of shoes, *you are dipping into your own fortune.* I once had a woman tell me she was so angry at her philandering husband that she charged $18,000 worth of new clothes on his credit card the week before the divorce. I had to remind her that 50 cents of every dollar her husband made was hers. She might have thought she was spending his paycheck, but actually she was spending her own!

MYTH #4: The excitement dies as the marriage lasts.

This does not have to be true. Treat your marriage as an investment and it will pay off. Don't ignore the benefits and the real worth just because partners are familiar and you see them every day. Remember: a strong family dynasty will come from a long-lasting marriage. It's an axiom that is as true of money as it is of partnerships: what you pay attention to will grow.

THE GOOD NEWS:
YOUR FAMILY DYNASTY AND YOUR
FINANCIAL LEGACY

Love. Marriage. Kids. These are the rites of passage that mark the most important parts of our lives. At our core we all want the same thing: safety and stability, happiness, a good life for our family. Money simply funds these fundamental desires, and without it, life just isn't going to be as fulfilling.

In this book, I've given you tips and strategies to grow your money and your relationships. I've shown you how to navigate the tricky world of dating and choose a mate with whom you are financially compatible. You now have tools for treating your partnership like a business, for doing due diligence on any potential life partners and for sticking to a budget once you commit to a life together. If you have children, I hope they've benefited from this book, too, whether they are still in the process of getting their O'Leary "MBA" or cruising into their 20s and heading for the world of work and dynasty-building for themselves. If your partnership has suffered some financial blows and you're considering divorce—that costly dissolution of your family dynasty that penalizes you and makes others rich—I've urged you to consider your options carefully. But if you were already divorced when you picked up this book, don't lose hope. You are now armed with knowledge for building a stronger partnership, one that can withstand the test of time.

My goal has always been to help you preserve your dynasty. I never said I was going to make you a multimillionaire, but you've got a better chance at that if you follow the advice in this book. What I truly want is to help you get to a place of financial safety. Having money means having freedom—the freedom to live the life you want to live. It means putting your kids through school so they can live out their passions and their dreams. It means knowing you can support yourself in your golden years, without having to be a burden on others. Financial security might even mean realizing a lifelong aspiration.

It's a magical night at our cottage on the lake in Muskoka. Linda is sitting beside me on the dock, Savannah and Trevor across from us. We've uncorked a bottle of O'Leary unoaked chardonnay, one of my favorites. Trevor is softly playing his guitar; Savannah is telling us a funny story about one of her university professors. The cottage is our family refuge, a symbol of the security, wealth and freedom of our dynasty. We're enjoying each other's company, talking, laughing, the moon full in the evening sky.

Imagine yourself in your family's safe haven, surrounded by your family dynasty, big or small. Your business or career is thriving, your partnership is stronger than ever and you've put aside enough money to be well cared for until the end of your life. Best of all, your kids aren't entitled mooches—they are emerging toward financial independence, and even better, they're showing signs of wanting to carry on your legacy. Guess what? Your money is safe. Your kids are safe. Your partner is safe. Your future is safe. And you are also happy. Who says you can't have it all?

ACKNOWLEDGEMENTS

Many thanks to my collaborator Bree Barton and senior editor Nita Pronovost, who helped me write this book. Thanks also to Doubleday Canada, in particular Brad Martin, Kristin Cochrane and Josh Glover, and to my agent Mel Berger for being the best in the biz. I want to thank my father, George, who meticulously scrutinizes my written work, always for the better.

I started my journey decades ago with my wife, Linda. At our wedding reception, we could only afford pizza for our guests. She is pragmatic about money because we started with none. Much of the advice in this book about family financial matters comes from my experience watching her run our family. What she did worked.

Finally, I want to thank my children, Savannah and Trevor. I learn much from them. The world today is a very challenging place for young people. Watching them deal with the problems thrown at them as they make their transition into adulthood provided me with a treasure trove of inspiration for this book.

INDEX

capital gains tax, 254–55
cars
  as money pits, 15–16
  repossession, 46
Cash Curriculum, 119–37
Catastrophe Cash Fund, 102,
    193
Cato (Roman statesman), 62–63
children. *See also* teenagers
  accidental pregnancy, 177–78
  adoption, 164–65
  bringing to work, 126–27
  and budgeting, 124–25,
    136–37
  as caregivers for parents,
    232–33
  Cash Curriculum, 119–37
  cost of raising, 105–9, 166–69,
    178
  and debit cards, 130–31
  and earning money, 122–24,
    129, 131–32
  educating about money,
    117–42
  and financial planners,
    134–35
  historical role of, 61–62
  instilling values in, 138–40
  and jobs, 143–57

  and saving, 120–22
  spoiling, 160–62
Chilton, David, 102
Christmas presents, 162
clothing, 17–18, 167–68, 193
cohabitation, 22
cohabitation agreements, 258
"cold hard cash" careers, 181–86
collection agencies, 45, 46, 77
Comeau, Elaine Tan, 214–17
common-law relationships,
    88–92, 257–58
community involvement, 72
compound interest, on credit
    cards, 174–77
courtship, 13, 20–23, 28–42
credit cards, 45–46
  interest, 174–77
credit rating, 45, 47, 172–74
cremation, 236
Critical 10, 231

dating, 11–27
  inexpensively, 24–27
  money leaks, 15–20
  online, 18–20, 26–27, 64
death, planning for, 41–42,
    224–26, 235–37, 238–40
debit cards, 130–31

debt
  borrowing from friends or
    family, 44–45
  and choosing a mate, 42
  credit card, 45–46, 174–77
  and midlife crises, 248
  mortgages, 101–3
  timeline for paying down,
    249–50
Denise Decree, 241–43
dining out, 16–17, 25–26
  "Kids Eat Free" nights, 169
diversification
  of financial advisors, 85
  financial independence and,
    80
  in investing, 81, 82
dividend-paying securities,
    82–83, 134–35
divorce, 251–59
  cost, 243–45, 252
  division of assets, 254–55
  90-Day Cool-Down, 253
  shadow, 253–55, 257
divorce rate, 12, 32, 64, 66, 255–56
drug use, 179–81, 246–47
due diligence, and relation-
    ships, 12–14, 19–23, 31–38,
    65–66, 68–70

Dyer, Anna, 221
Dyer, Rob, 217–21

Easy Daysies Ltd., 214–17
education
  graduate degrees, 197–98
  to learn a trade, 181–86
  and marital success, 72–73
  saving for, 108
employers
  pension plans, 192–93
  and social media, 194–97
estate planning, 238–40
E.T.s (Entrepreneurs in
    Training), 131–32, 141–42
exercise, 24, 71–72

Family Bank Day, 121–22
family businesses, 90–92, 207–23
  avoiding "yes men," 221
  business family tree, 222–23
  involving friends in, 217–20
  monetizing unique skills, 220
  relationships with clients,
    216–17
  research, 215–16
  sacrifices required, 212–13
  setting financial benchmarks,
    212

I love great wine, and I never spend money
without looking for great value.

If you share these ideals, then I think you'll love
O'Leary Fine Wines as much as I do. Cheers!

Kevin O'Leary

Learn more at
kevinoleary.com/finewines

Copyright © O'Leary Ventures Corporation. Trademarks used under
license by Vineland Estates Winery. Enjoy responsibly.

Don't let your mortgage
take a bite out of you.

Get O'Leary
on your side.

O'LEARY
MORTGAGES.COM

Learn more at **olearymortgages.com**

See website for details.

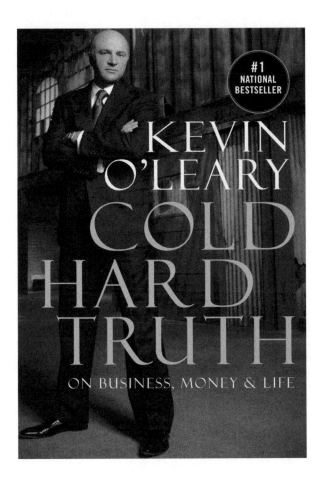

#1
NATIONAL
BESTSELLER

KEVIN
O'LEARY
COLD
HARD
TRUTH

ON BUSINESS, MONEY & LIFE

"O'Leary's book reads exactly like he talks on *Dragons' Den*. . . .
If you're an aspiring entrepreneur or someone who's debating
whether to pursue your passion, you'll get some invaluable advice."
The Hamilton Spectator

"Candour is Kevin O'Leary's specialty and his strongest selling point."
The Globe and Mail

Available wherever books are sold

ANCHOR CANADA
www.randomhouse.ca

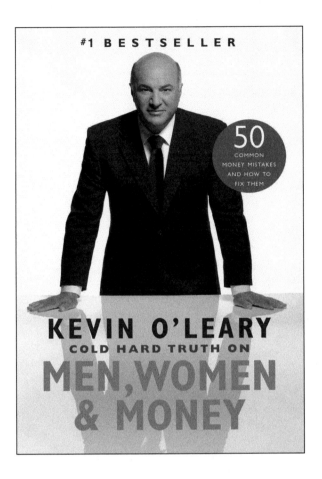

#1 BESTSELLER

50
COMMON
MONEY MISTAKES
AND HOW TO
FIX THEM

KEVIN O'LEARY
COLD HARD TRUTH ON
MEN, WOMEN
& MONEY

"Stressed out about the grown child who won't leave your basement? Have family members circling like vultures now that you're retired and saved your nest egg? Unable to climb out of debt? As if he were the Don Cherry of financial wisdom, O'Leary provides strongly worded, anecdote-driven answers, unafraid of the people he might offend."
National Post

Available wherever books are sold

ANCHOR CANADA
www.randomhouse.ca